M000276960

Sputnik: An Introductory Russian Language Course, Part I
ISBN: 978-0-9939139-0-7

Preface

Sputnik: *An introductory Russian language course* is designed with focused attention to the development of each language skill: reading, writing, listening and communication.
The course consists of the textbook, workbook and the website www.sputniktextbook.org.

The textbook offers various classroom activities, grammar explanations, basic active vocabulary and authentic reading materials. It provides students with a step-by-step introduction to pronunciation through the sequence of carefully selected exercises on reading syllables, words and short sentences, all accompanied by recorded sounds.

The workbook includes exercises which encourage students to use what they are learning in class through writing meaningful and practical texts (from short notes to a Russian friend to recommendations and academic background descriptions). It also teaches students how to write in cursive Russian.

The website provides:

- a range of audio materials recorded by professional Russian actors and announcers;
- interactive homework exercises and grammar drills;
- automatic checking and grading of online activities;
- an interface for the instructor to monitor students' online activity and progress.

Acknowledgements and credits

The author is pleased to express her gratitude to all the wonderful professionals who contributed their knowledge and skills to this project and without whom it would not be possible to create a modern textbook.

Publishing Director: Michael Skrigitil
Editor: Carolyn Pytlyk
Book Illustrator: Natalia Gavrilova
Book Designer: Elena Pushkina
Sound Director: Elena Rumyantseva

Actors and Announcers:
Maria Dodenkova
Lyubov Litova
Natalia Nikitina
Aleksei Leonov
Denis Garmash
Evgeniy Rozhko

We are thankful to all instructors and students who piloted this textbook in their Russian language classes. A special thank you to instructors of Russian who took time to review the textbook and give us valuable feedback:

Elena Bratishenko, University of Calgary
Olga Mladenova, University of Calgary
Dorotka Lockyer, University of Victoria
Zsuzsa Szabo-Nyarady, University of New Brunswuick

Their insightful comments and suggestions have been very helpful.

Photo Credits: Photographs are taken from the Wikimedia Commons (Images) and released into the public domain. Photo details are provided on page 231.

Table of Contents

Тема 1. Буквы и звуки
Introduction to Russian Letters and Sounds

Практика. Фонетика. Интонация

- Russian letters and sounds. **Алфави́т**
- Stress in and vowel reduction in Russian
- Intonation in statements and yes-no questions: **ИК-1** and **ИК-3**
- Intonation in statements: **ИК-1** and **ИК-3** for listing
- Intonation in questions with question words: **ИК-2**
- Hard and soft consonants
- Vowel reduction: letters **о**, **а**, **е**, **я**
- Asking for additional information: **ИК-4**
- Voiced and voiceless consonants
- Formal and informal conversations
- Russian names: **и́мя**, **о́тчество**, **фами́лия**
- Counting in Russian

Грамматика

- Statements and questions. The verb *to be* in present tense
- Gender of nouns and pronouns. Introduction

Культура

- Russian alphabet. A brief history

Читаем и понимаем

- Reading Russian tongue twisters and poems

Алфавит

The modern Russian Alphabet has 33 characters: 21 consonant letters, 10 vowel letters and 2 signs (hard and soft). Reading in Russian is easy once you have learned the letters and simple pronunciation rules.

Слу́шайте и повторя́йте. Listen and repeat. Listen to your teacher and the recordings, and then imitate them as closely as you can.

Буква Letter	Звук Sound similar to
А а	**ar** in f**ar**
Б б	**b** in **b**ox
В в	**v** in **v**oice
Г г	**g** in **g**o
Д д	**d** in **d**ay
Е е	**ye** in **ye**llow or **e** in **e**xit
Ё ё	**yo** in **yo**ghurt
Ж ж	**s** in plea**s**ure
З з	**z** in **z**oo
И и	**ee** in ch**ee**se
Й й	**y** in bo**y**
К к	**k** in **k**ey
Л л	**l** in **l**amp
М м	**m** in **m**an
Н н	**n** in **n**ote
О о	**o** in n**o**t
П п	**p** in **p**et

Буква Letter	Звук Sound similar to
Р р	**r** in **r**ock (but rolled)
С с	**s** in **s**un
Т т	**t** in **t**ea
У у	**oo** in m**oo**n
Ф ф	**f** in **f**ood
Х х	**ch** in Scottish lo**ch**
Ц ц	**ts** in ca**ts**
Ч ч	**ch** in **ch**at
Ш ш	**sh** in **sh**ort
Щ щ	**shch** in fre**sh ch**eese
ъ	no sound
ы	**i** in **i**ll
ь	no sound
Э э	**e** in **e**nd
Ю ю	like **u** in **u**se
Я я	like **ya** in **ya**rd

Урок 1

Russian orthography (i.e., the rules of how the letters represent the sounds of a language) is more transparent than English. That means, it is quite easy to predict the pronunciation of a word based on how it is written.

Since Russian words are generally longer and they change their forms, the approach to reading in Russian is different from reading in English. In Russian, you should learn to read words by syllables. Each syllable is a combination of a consonant or consonants and a single vowel). Once you've mastered syllable reading, you should be able to read longer words without difficulty

.

1.1–1. Слу́шайте и повторя́йте. Practice reading the letters and syllables below.

Vowels А а О о У у Э э and Consonants М м П п Б б

а — о — у — э	э — у — о — а	
ма — мо — му — мэ	па — по — пу — пэ	ба — бо — бу — бэ
ам — ом — ум — эм	ап — оп — уп — эп	

Consonants Н н Т т Д д

на — но — ну — нэ	та — то — ту — тэ	да — до — ду — дэ
ан — он — ун — эн	ат — от — ут — эт	

1.1–2. Слу́шайте и повторя́йте.

ма́ма	па́па	ба́ба	ду́ма	дом	мо́да
mom	*dad*	*granny*	*thought*	*house*	*fashion*
бана́н	ум	тут	там	том	Эмма
banana	*mind*	*here*	*there*	*volume*	*Emma*

1.1-3. Слу́шайте и чита́йте. Listen to the sentences and read them aloud.

Тут ма́ма.

Там па́па.

Там дом.

Тут бана́н.

Stress and Vowel Reduction in Russian

Stress

The little symbol on top of a vowel letter is a stress mark. It shows the "strong" syllable in a word. In the word **мо́да**, the syllable **мо́** is stressed and in the word **бана́н**, the second syllable **а́н** is stressed. The stressed syllable is pronounced with stronger emphasis on the vowel. Listen to the words on the previous page again and pronounce them with emphasis on the stressed syllable.

It is important to memorize stress as part of the pronunciation of a given word. Stress affects the way certain vowels are pronounced and distinguishes otherwise identical words. Repeat after your instructor and compare:

до́ма — дома́	*at home — houses*
То́ма — тома́	*girl's name — volumes*

Stress is marked in dictionaries and texts for language learners. Original Russian publications do not mark stress. As you make progress in Russian, you will remember how words sound and will not need stress marks. In this text, the stress is marked for all Russian words with the following exceptions.

If a word has only one vowel (like **дом**, **там**, **ум**), there is no stress mark placed on it.

Stress is not marked on capitalized vowels. If you see a name like **Анна** with no stress mark, you know to place stress on the first **А**. This applies to proper names and words that begin a sentence.

Vowel Reduction

Some Russian vowels sound differently when not stressed. This change in the pronunciation of an unstressed vowel is called **vowel reduction**. It is most noticeable with the pronunciation of Russian **o** which is reduced to the sound of [**a**] in **a***bove* (marked in transcription as [**ə**]) when not stressed.

1.1–4. Слу́шайте и повторя́йте. Unstressed vowel **o** sounds like [**ə**].

дома́	тома́	а́том	пото́м	э́то	он	она́	оно́
houses	*volumes*	*atom*	*later*	*this is*	*he*	*she*	*it*

1.1–5. Слу́шайте и повторя́йте.

Consonants С с З з Ф ф В в

са — со — су — сэ   фа — фо — фу — фэ

ас — ос — ус — эс   аф — оф — уф — эф

за — зо — зу — зэ   ва — во — ву — вэ

> Note: Russian **С с** sounds like [**s**] in ***S****am* (never like [**k**]).

1.1–6. Слу́шайте и повторя́йте. Remember to emphasize stressed vowels and reduce the unstressed **o** vowels to [**ə**].

сова́	вас	зову́т	ва́нна	ва́за	фонта́н
owl	*a form of "you"*	*they call*	*bathtub*	*vase*	*fountain*
вода́	суп	вот	оса́	сон	фо́то
water	*soup*	*here (it) is*	*wasp*	*dream*	*photo*

Consonants К к Г г Х х

К к sounds like [**k**] in ***k****ey* or [**c**] in ***c****at*. Russian has one letter to represent the sound [**k**].

Г г sounds like [**g**] in ***G****avin*.

Х х sounds like [**ch**] in *lo**ch*** and *Ba**ch***. You may need same extra practice pronouncing this sound.

1.1–7. Слу́шайте и повторя́йте. Practice reading these "back consonants". Note how all three are formed with the back of your tongue.

ка — ко — ку — кэ   ха — хо — ху — хэ   га — го — гу — гэ

ак — ок — ук — эк   ах — ох — ух — эх

1.1–8. Слу́шайте и повторя́йте.

как	когда́	кто	кот	у́хо	уха́	э́хо
how	*when*	*who*	*cat*	*ear*	*fresh fish soup*	*echo*
окно́	а́вгуст	нога́	соба́ка	бу́ква	звук	сок
window	*August*	*leg*	*dog*	*letter*	*sound*	*juice*

1.1–9. Слу́шайте и чита́йте. Listen to the sentences and read them aloud.

Это кот.

Это соба́ка.

Это оса́.

Там сова́.

Это бу́ква А.

Это окно́.

Вот фонта́н. Там вода́.

1.1–10. Слу́шайте и повторя́йте. Ри́тмика. The rhythm of Russian words. Practice reading the following short words, emphasizing each stressed syllable.

—	⁄— —	— ⁄—
дом	дома	дома
ум	Тома	тома
тут	мама	банан
там	папа	потом
том	дума	она
он	мода	оно
вас	атом	они
суп	это	сова
сон	ванна	зовут
вот	ваза	фонтан
как	фото	вода
кот	эхо	оса
кто	ухо	уха
звук	август	окно
сок	буква	нога
		когда

Statements and Questions. The Verb *to be* in Present Tense

Short statements and questions are easy to form in Russian because the verb *to be* is absent in present tense. To make it even easier for you, Russian has no articles, *a*, *an*, and *the*. Compare the Russian and English statements and questions below.

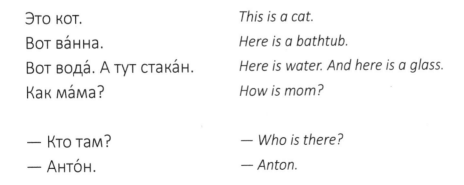

Это кот.	*This is a cat.*
Вот ва́нна.	*Here is a bathtub.*
Вот вода́. А тут стака́н.	*Here is water. And here is a glass.*
Как ма́ма?	*How is mom?*
— Кто там?	*— Who is there?*
— Анто́н.	*— Anton.*

1.1–11. Make up your own sentences in Russian. Look at the pictures, and say what you see.

Это ... Это ... Это ... А тут ...

1.1–12. Читайте. Remember to emphasize stressed vowels and reduce the unstressed **о** vowels to [**ə**].

Это дом. А вот окнó.

Это мáма, а э́то пáпа.

Тут вáза, а там водá. Вот стакáн.

Это бýква О, а э́то бýква У.

Жизнь в Росси́и: лю́ди, исто́рия, культу́ра
Russian Alphabet. A Brief History

Russian is an Eastern Slavonic language closely related to Ukrainian and Belorussian with about 277 million speakers in Russia and 30 other countries.

The Russian alphabet uses the Cyrillic script, which is named after the Byzantine scholar and monk, Cyril (827-869 AD). Cyril and his brother Methodius (826-885 AD) created the first Slavic writing system in the second half of the 9th century.

Cyril and Methodius were two Byzantine (half Greek, half Slavic) brothers born in Thessaloniki in the 9th century. They became missionaries of Christianity and created the first Slavic writing system in order to translate the Bible and other Christian texts into the Slavic languages.

Глаго́лица. The Glagolitic Alphabet

The alphabet created by Cyril was called **Глаго́лица** (*Glagolitsa*). The Glagolitic Alphabet is the oldest known Slavic alphabet. It looks very different from the Cyrillic Alphabet.

The Glagolitic Alphabet

The name of this earliest alphabet comes from the Old Slavic *glagolŭ* meaning "sound". The Glagolitic Alphabet was used for Slavonic manuscripts for approximately a century before it was gradually replaced by the Cyrillic Alphabet.

Кири́ллица. The Cyrillic Alphabet

The earliest form of **Кири́ллица**, the Cyrillic Alphabet (also known as Азбука, from the old name of the first two letters, and Bulgarian Alphabet) was based on Greek script with a few letters adapted from the Glagolitic Alphabet to use for the sounds not found in Greek. It was introduced by Cyril's pupils who named it after their teacher. Variations of the Cyrillic Alphabet are used by a variety of Slavic languages — Belarusian, Bulgarian, Macedonian, Russian, Serbian, and Ukrainian.

Before the 17th century, the only written language in Russia was Old Church Slavonic. Monasteries were the centres of education.

Civil Russian language first appeared in writing during the reign of Peter the Great (1672-1725), who introduced a revised and shortened alphabet. He also encouraged authors to use a writing style closer to their spoken language. Peter was the one who made the final choices of future civil letter-forms: he crossed out the ones that were unappealling from a set of charts presented to him. From early 18th century onward Peter's revised alphabet was used to write civil texts (science, commerce, correspondence, civil literary texts, etc.) while the original Old Church Slavonic script remained in writings related to the Orthodox religion.

The Original Cyrillic Alphabet

Charts with letters crossed out by Peter I

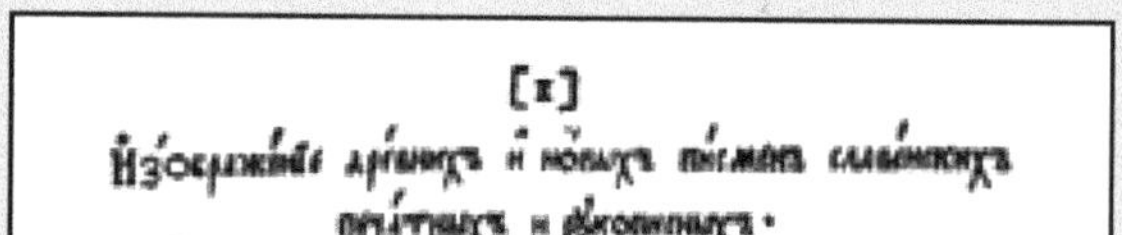

Russian alphabet was last revised during the language reform in 1917/18, eliminating four more letters from the alphabet.

Урок 2

This lesson introduces new letters that sound quite different from their English counterparts.

Consonants Л л Р р

Russian **Л л** is pronounced differently from English **L l**. To say **л**, press your tongue against upper teeth.

1.2–1. Слу́шайте и повторя́йте. Practice pronouncing **Л л** in the two-, three-, and four-letter syllables below.

ла — ло — лу — лэ	бла — пла — сла — зла	бло — пло — сло — зло
ал — ол — ул — эл	алк — олк — улк — элк	гла — гло — глу

ла — пла — спла	ло — кло — скло
ла — гла — мгла	лу — глу — вглу

Russian **Р р** differs from that of the English sound represented by [**r**] in ***rocket*** but is very similar to the rolled [**r**] in Spanish.

1.2–2. Слу́шайте и повторя́йте. Practice pronouncing **Р р** in the two-, three-, and four-letter syllables below.

ра — ро — ру — рэ	бра — пра — дра — тра	бро — про — дро — тро
ар — ор — ур — эр	арк — орк — урк	арт — орт — урн
дра — дро — дру	тра — тро — тру	

ра — дра — здра	ро — бро — збро	ру — дру — вдру
ра — тра — стра	ро — про — спро	ру — тру — стру

1.2–3. Слу́шайте и повторя́йте. Remember to emphasize stressed vowels and reduce the unstressed **о** vowels to [**ə**].

ма́сло	слова́	голова́	молоко́	бума́га	ла́мпа	
butter	*words*	*head*	*milk*	*paper*	*lamp*	
рука́	са́хар	доро́га	пра́вда	тру́дно	вопро́с	уро́к
hand	*sugar*	*road*	*truth*	*it is difficult*	*question*	*lesson*

Vowels И и vs. ы

Russian **И и** is similar to English [**ee**] in ***meet*** but shorter in length.

1.2–4. Слу́шайте и повторя́йте. Practice pronouncing **И и** in the following syllables.

ти — ди — ни — ми　　ли — ри — би — пи

им — ин — ит — их　　ил — ир — ип — ик

Russian **ы** is similar to English **i** in *h**i**ll* and *b**i**ll*. This little trick will help you properly articulate the sound of **ы**: try to say English **u** (like the one in *p**u**t*) and smile at the exact same time. The letter **ы** never starts a word, and therefore is not capitalized.

1.2–5. Слу́шайте и повторя́йте. Practice pronouncing **ы** in the syllables below.

ты — ды — мы — ны　　сы — зы — бы — пы

лы — ры — вы — фы

1.2–6. Слу́шайте и повторя́йте. Pay attention to different pronunciation of **И и** and **ы**.

и	мир	си́ла	кни́га	рис	лимо́н	и́ли
and	*world, peace*	*power*	*book*	*rice*	*lemon*	*or*
ты	мы	вы	сын	сыр	ры́ба	бана́ны
you	*we*	*you (plural)*	*son*	*cheese*	*fish*	*bananas*

сын — си́ла　　ры́ба — рис — сыр　　вы — и — мы

1.2–7. Чита́йте. Remember to emphasize stressed vowels and reduce the unstressed **o** vowels to [**ə**].

Мы за мир.

We are for peace.

Ми́ру — мир!

To the world — peace!

Ма́ма, па́па и их сын Анто́н ходи́ли в магази́н.

Mom, dad and their son Anton went shopping.

Ма́ма купи́ла ма́сло, рис и сыр.

Mom bought butter, rice and cheese.

Па́па купи́л кни́ги.

Dad bought books.

А их сын Анто́н купи́л фотоаппара́т.

And their son Anton bought a camera.

Intonation in Statements and Yes-No Questions: ИК-1 and ИК-3

Unlike English, Russian yes-no questions (questions without a question word) have the exact same structure as simple statements.

Это кни́га.	*This is a book.*
Это кни́га?	*Is this a book?*

Since the sentence structure is the same, Russian uses intonation to distinguish yes-no questions from simple statements.

ИК-1[1] is used in declarative statements. It is marked by a drop of the tone on the centre of the **ИК-1**. The centre of the **ИК-1** is the stressed syllable of the word containing the main information.

ИК-3 is used in yes-no questions. It is marked by sharp rise of the tone on the centre of **ИК-3**. The centre of **ИК-3** is the stressed syllable of the word in question.

1.2–8. Слу́шайте и повторя́йте. Pay attention to different intonation in **ИК-1** and **ИК-3**.

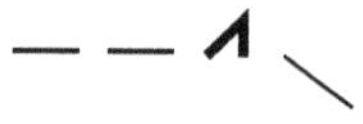 **ИК-3**

Это кни́га?

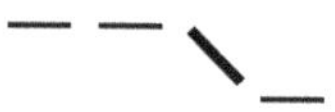 **ИК-1**

Это кни́га.

ИК-3	ИК-1
Это пра́вда?	Это пра́вда.
Это тру́дно?	Это тру́дно.
Ма́ма до́ма?	Она́ до́ма.
Анто́н до́ма?	Он до́ма.
— Это сыр?	— Да, э́то сыр.
— Это рис?	— Да, э́то рис.
— Это бума́га?	— Да, э́то бума́га.
— Тут са́хар?	— Да, са́хар.
— Там молоко́?	— Да, молоко́.

1 **ИК** is common abbreviation for Интоннационная конструкция (*Intonation contour*). This section introduces four basic Intonation contours: **ИК-1**, **ИК-2**, **ИК-3**, and **ИК-4**.

Hushing Consonants Ш ш and Ж ж

Ш ш is similar to English **sh** in ***sh**arp*.
Ж ж sounds like the middle of *plea**s**ure* or the end of *gara**g**e*.

1.2–9. Слу́шайте и повторя́йте. Practice pronouncing **Ш ш** and **Ж ж** in the syllables below.

ша — шо — шу	жа — жо — жу	жо — шо
аш — ош — уш — эш	жа — ша	жу — шу

1.2–10. Слу́шайте и повторя́йте. Remember to emphasize stressed vowels and reduce the unstressed **o** vowels to [**ə**].

шарф	ша́пка	шо́рты	шко́ла	шу́тка	хорошо́
scarf	*hat*	*shorts*	*school*	*joke*	*well done*
журна́л	жа́рко	дру́жба	мо́жно	ну́жно	ва́жно
journal	*it's hot*	*friendship*	*may*	*need*	*important*

> Note: the letter **и** sounds like [**ы**] after **ж** and **ш**.
> Always write **жи**, **ши** but say [**жы**], [**шы**].

1.2–11. Слу́шайте и повторя́йте. Pay attention to pronunciation of **жи** and **ши**.

маши́на	карандаши́	у́ши	су́ши	Пиши́!
car	*pencils*	*ears*	*sushi*	*Write!*
они́ жи́ли	живо́т	лы́жи	Скажи́	у́жин
they lived	*stomach*	*ski*	*Tell me*	*supper*

1.2–12. Чита́йте. Pay attention to pronunciation and spelling of **жи** and **ши**.

Ма́ша, вот бума́га и карандаши́. Пиши́: «лы́жи, маши́на». Запо́мни: «жи» и «ши» пиши́ с «и».

Хорошо́, Ма́ша!

запо́мни — *remember*

Hushing Consonants Ч ч and Щ щ

Ч ч is similar to English **ch** in ***ch**at* and ***ch**eese*.

Щ щ has no equivalent in English; the closest sound is the English combination **shch** in *fre**sh** **ch**eese*.

1.2–13. Слу́шайте и повторя́йте. Practice pronouncing **Ч ч** and **Щ щ** in the following syllables.

ча — чо — чу — чи	ща — що — щу — щи	ча — ща	чу — щу
ач — оч — уч — ич	ащ — ощ — ущ — ищ	чо — що	чи — щи

1.2–14. Слу́шайте и повторя́йте. Pay attention to pronunciation of **Ч ч** and **Щ щ**.

час	ча́сто	очки́	ру́чка	врач	Учи́!
hour	*often*	*glasses*	*pen*	*doctor*	*Learn!*
борщ	щи	о́вощи	плащ	защи́та	това́рищ
borsch	*cabbage soup*	*vegetables*	*raincoat*	*defense*	*comrade*

1.2–15. Слу́шайте и повторя́йте. Pay attention to the intonation: sharp rise of the tone on the centre of **ИК-3** and a drop of the tone on the centre of the **ИК-1**. Remember to emphasize stressed vowels and reduce the unstressed **о** vowels to [ə]. Read left to right.

3	1	3	1
Это нужно?	Это нужно.	Это важно?	Это важно.
3	1 1	3	1
— Это школа?	Да, это школа.	Можно каранда́ш?	Можно.

1.2–16. Чита́йте. Remember to emphasize stressed vowels and reduce the unstressed **o** vowels to [ə].

У нас на у́жин ры́ба и су́ши.

For supper we are having fish and sushi.

А у нас на у́жин ча́сто борщ и о́вощи.

And we often have borsch and veggies for supper.

Ма́ша у́чит слова́.

Masha is learning words.

Са́ша, вот бума́га и ру́чка. Пиши́ бу́квы и слова́.

Sasha, here is paper and a pen. Write letters and words.

Reading Long Words

Russian has many long words that are not easy to read. When you come across a long word, try to break it into syllables and read syllables slowly connecting them into one word. This is the way Russian children learn how to read. Their first books have long words broken into syllables.

1.2–17. Чита́йте. Try this simple trick to handle long words with ease. Read this short text aloud. Remember to emphasize stressed vowels and reduce the unstressed **o** vowels to [ə].

Вот бу-ма́-га и ру́-чка. Са́-ша, за-пи-ши́ и за-по́-мни сло-ва́: ба́-бу-шка, то-ва́-рищ, о́-во-щи, ка-ра-нда-ши́, фо-то-а-ппа-ра́т.

запиши́ — *write down*

1.2–18. Слу́шайте и повторя́йте. Ри́тмика. The rhythm of Russian words. Practice reading various rhythmic patterns of words. Remember to emphasize stressed vowels and reduce the unstressed **о** vowels to [ə].

—	—́ —	— —́	—́ — —	— —́ —	— — —́
суп	мама	банан	овощи	собака	голова
кот	папа	сова	бабушка	бананы	молоко
сок	ухо	зовут		товарищ	запиши
рис	масло	оса		запомни	
сын	сахар	уха			
сыр	рыба	нога			
шарф	шапка	рука			
врач	шорты	лимон			
борщ	уши	пиши			
щи	суши	скажи			
плащ	дочка	учи			

1.2–19. Group the words from the previous exercise into categories: people, animals, foods, body parts, clothing, and commands. Put stress marks on words.

Лю́ди — People:

____

____

Живо́тные — Animals (includes birds and insects):

Еда́ — Foods:

Те́ло — Body:

Оде́жда — Clothing:

Кома́нды — Commands:

Урок 3

Consonants Ц ц and Й й

Ц ц is similar to English **ts** in *ca**ts*** and *pe**ts***.

Й й is called **и**-краткое or “short **и**”. It is pronounced similar to English **y** in *to**y*** and *bo**y***.

1.3–1. Слу́шайте и повторя́йте. Practice pronouncing **Ц ц** and **Й й** in these syllables.

ца — цо — цу — ци   ай — уй — ый — ий

ац — оц — уц — иц   ой — йо

1.3–2. Слу́шайте и повторя́йте. Pay attention to pronunciation of **Ц ц** and **Й й**.

лицо́	цирк	ци́фра	у́лица	столи́ца	
face	*circus*	*number, digit*	*street*	*capital*	
йо́гурт	мой	твой	чай	ча́йник	Дай!
yogurt	*my*	*yours*	*tea*	*teapot*	*Give!*

1.3–3. Слу́шайте и повторя́йте. Pay attention to intonation: **ИК-3** for yes-no questions and **ИК-1** for simple statements.

— Это твой (3) йо́гурт?   — Да, мой (1).

— Это цирк (3)?   — Да, э́то (1) цирк.

1.3–4. Чита́йте. Remember to emphasize stressed vowels and reduce the unstressed **o** vowels to [ə].

Москва́ — столи́ца Росси́и.

Вашингто́н — столи́ца США*.

Ло́ндон — столи́ца Англии.

Отта́ва — столи́ца Кана́ды.

Intonation in Statements: ИК-1 and ИК-3 for Listing

When you list things in Russian, **ИК-3** is used for each item in a series. The final item of the series is marked by **ИК-1**.

1.3–5. Слу́шайте и повторя́йте.

ИК-3	ИК-3	ИК-3	ИК-1
Вот кни́га,	бума́га,	каранда́ш	и ру́чка.

* США (Соединённые Шта́ты Аме́рики) — *USA (United States of America)*

1.3–6. Слу́шайте и повторя́йте. Pay attention to intonation: **ИК-3** for each item in a series and **ИК-1** for final item of the series.

Ма́ма купи́ла масло[3], молоко[3], сыр[3], йогурт[3] и чай[1].

Па́па купи́л книги[3], журнал[3], карандаш[3] и очки[1].

Анто́н купи́л лыжи[3], шарф[3] и фотоаппарат[1].

1.3–7. Чита́йте. Pay attention to intonation while reading aloud.

— Са́ша, вот чайник[1].

— Там чай[3]?

— Да, чай[1]. Вот чашка[1]. Тут молоко[3], сахар[3], сыр[3], масло[3] и тост[1]. А вот йогурт[1].

— Спасибо[1].

— Пожалуйста[1].

— Дай, пожа́луйста, карандаш[1].

Give me the pencil, please.

— Вот, пожалуйста[1].

Here it is. (= Please take it.)

Пожа́луйста (pronounced as [**пажа́лста**]) means *"You are welcome"* and is commonly used as a response to **Спаси́бо!** *"Thank you"*. It is also used as *"please"*.

Vowels Е е Ё ё Ю ю Я я

These four letters are pronounced as two sounds similar to English **ye** in ***ye**llow*, **yo** in ***yo**ghurt*, **yu** in ***u**se*, and **ya** in ***ya**rd* in the positions listed below:

- at the beginning of the word,
- after another vowel, and
- after **ь** and **ъ** signs.

1.3–8. Слу́шайте и повторя́йте.

я — ё — ю — е   е — ю — ё — я

моя́	моё	твоя́	твоё	я	ёлка
my (f)	*my (n)*	*yours (f)*	*yours(n)*	*I*	*fir tree*
я́блоко	статья́	объе́кт	Юлия	Яна	Зо́я
apple	*article*	*object*	*Yulia*	*Yana*	*Zoya*

The letter **Ё ё** is always stressed; therefore, the stress on words that have this letter is not marked.
Most Russian publications do not mark dots on top of **Ё ё**. This makes the letter look exactly like **Е е**. Russians simply know where to say ***ye*** and where to say ***yo***.

Gender of Nouns and Pronouns. Introduction

Russian nouns belong to one of the three genders: masculine, feminine, or neuter. The gender is easy to tell by looking at the noun's ending. Compare Russian and English phrases below and tell what grammatical distinctions you noticed.

Где мой каранда́ш? — Вот он. *Where is my pencil? — There it is.*

Где моя́ ру́чк**а**? — Вот он**а́**. *Where is my pen? — There it is.*

Где моё я́блок**о**? — Вот он**о́**. *Where is my apple? — There it is.*

Following this pattern, answer the questions in Russian using the correct form for *it*:

Где мой журна́л? — Вот ....

Где моя́ кни́га? — Вот ....

Где моё молоко́? — Вот ....

As you noticed, Russian has three different forms of *it*. The pronoun used to replace a noun depends on the gender of the noun.

он for a masculine noun (also means *he* when used for a person).
онá for a feminine noun (also means *she* when used for a person).
онó for a neuter noun (cannot be used for a person).

Note how pronouns endings match with nouns endings:

Ø stands for "no vowel"

masculine:	Ø	карандáш, журнáл — он
feminine:	а	рýчка, кни́га — онá
neuter:	о	я́блоко, молокó — онó

Russian words for *my* and *your* have different forms to match with the gender of a noun:

masculine:	**мой** карандáш, **твой** журнáл
feminine:	**моя́** рýчка, **твоя́** кни́га
neuter:	**моё** я́блоко, **твоё** молокó

You will learn more about grammatical gender in Тема 2.

Поговори́м! Let's talk!

1.3–9. А. You are in a hurry and cannot find your things today. Working with a partner, ask where they are. Here is what you need to find in the room: карандáш, рýчка, я́блоко, шарф, фотоаппарáт, чáшка. Your partner should point to the items on the picture below and say *Here it is...* in Russian, using the correct gender pronouns.

Образéц: Где мой журнáл? — Вот он.

Б. Now your friend is trying to find his/her things. Switch roles and help your friend finding these things: кни́га, собáка[3], банáн, молокó, йóгурт, шáпка in the same room.

3 The noun **собáка** — *dog* is feminine, regardless the physical gender of the dog.

Intonation in Questions with Question Words: ИК-2

Russian questions with question words are asked with a special intonation contour known as **ИК-2**. The centre of the **ИК-2** is stressed syllable of the question word. The tone drops sharply after the question word.

1.3–10. Слу́шайте и повторя́йте.

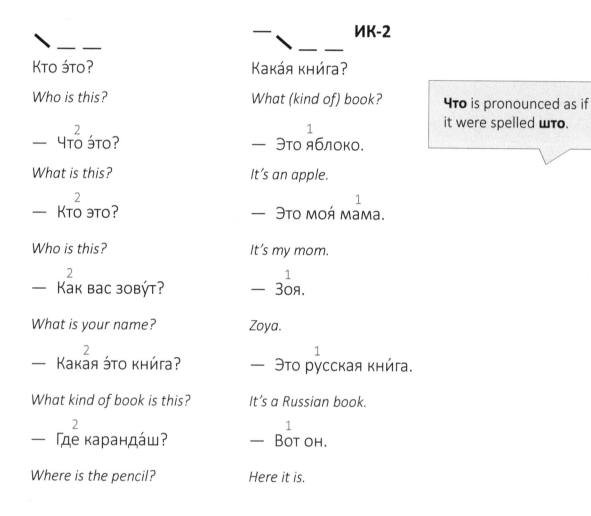

╲ — —	— ╲ — — **ИК-2**
Кто э́то?	Кака́я кни́га?
Who is this?	*What (kind of) book?*
— Что[2] э́то?	— Это я́блоко[1].
What is this?	*It's an apple.*
— Кто[2] это?	— Это моя́ мама[1].
Who is this?	*It's my mom.*
— Как[2] вас зову́т?	— Зоя[1].
What is your name?	*Zoya.*
— Какая[2] э́то кни́га?	— Это русская[1] кни́га.
What kind of book is this?	*It's a Russian book.*
— Где[2] каранда́ш?	— Вот[1] он.
Where is the pencil?	*Here it is.*

Что is pronounced as if it were spelled **што**.

ИК-2 is also used when you address someone or request something. Such sentences can have multiple **ИК** centres.

1.3–11. Слу́шайте и повторя́йте.

— Маша[2], скажи[2], что[2] это? — Это ру́сская книга[1].

Masha, tell me what is this? *It is a Russian book.*

— Маша[2], запомни[2], «жи» и «ши» пиши́[1] с «и».

Masha, remember: «жи» and «ши» write with «и».

1.3–12. Слу́шайте и повторя́йте. Интона́ция: ИК-1, ИК-2, ИК-3. Imitate the intonation patterns on the following questions as closely as you can.

ИК-1	ИК-2	ИК-3
Это кни́га.	Что э́то?	Это кни́га?
Это врач.	Кто э́то?	Это врач?
Ива́н врач.	Кто он?	Ива́н врач?
Ма́ма и па́па до́ма.	Кто до́ма?	Ма́ма и па́па до́ма?

Поговори́м!

1.3–13. Working with a partner, ask if you remember the Russian words for objects below. Ask the "wrong" question occasionally. Follow the model (Образе́ц) and remember to use proper intonation.

Образе́ц:

3
— Это собака?
1 1
— Да, э́то собака.

3
— Это собака?
1 1
— Нет, э́то кот.

Поговори́м!

1.3–14. You want to know the Russian words for objects below. Working with a partner, take turns asking questions **Кто э́то?** (*Who is this?*) and **Что э́то?** (*What is this?*) Follow the model (Образе́ц) and remember to use the proper intonation.

Образе́ц:

— Кто[2] это?

— Это соба[1]ка.

— Что[2] это?

— Это фонта[1]н.

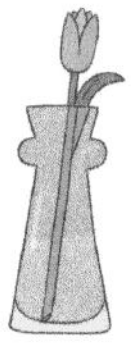

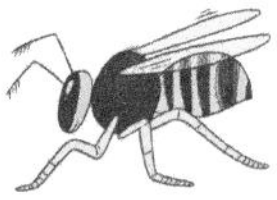

Поговори́м!

1.3–15. In groups of 4-6 students, ask each other's names: Как[2] вас зову́т?

Then, check if you remember all the names of the people in your group by asking:

— Это Э[3]лла?

Possible answers:

— Да[1], э́то Э[1]лла.

—Нет[1], э́то не Э[1]лла. Это А[1]нна.

> **Нет, э́то не** ...
> means *No, it's not...*

Урок 4

Hard and Soft Consonants

Most Russian consonant letters have two sounds: a hard and a soft sound. In the articulation of a hard consonant, the tongue is relaxed and not raised up. With the help of your instructor, practice saying the hard consonants: б, п, в, ф, д, т, л, м, н, р, з, с.

To articulate a soft consonant, raise the blade of your tongue up towards the roof of your mouth. It feels as if you are adding a very short ee-like sound while articulating the consonant. With the help of your instructor, practice saying these consonants softly: б', п', в', ф', д', т', л', м', н', р', з', с'.

The distinction between a hard and a soft can make a difference in the meaning of a word. With your instructor's help, practice saying the following pairs of words:

брат — брать	у́гол — у́голь	лук — люк
brother — to take	*corner — coal*	*onion — manhole*

Twelve Russian consonants can be either hard or soft: **Бб Вв Дд Зз Лл Мм Нн Пп Рр Сс Тт Фф**. The softness of a consonant is marked like this ['] in the phonetic transcription: thus, [брат'] is the transcription of брать.

1.4–1. Слу́шайте и повторя́йте. Practice pronouncing the pairs of syllables below to get used to the concept of hardness and softness of the consonants.

ба — бя	па — пя	за — зя	ва — вя
бо — бё	до — дё	ло — лё	фо — фё
бу — бю	су — сю	ру — рю	лу — лю
бэ — бе	рэ — ре	мэ — ме	сэ — се
бы — би	ты — ти	ны — ни	мы — ми

The Russian language has five vowel sounds but ten vowel letters. Letters in each pair: **а — я, о — ё, у — ю, э — е, ы — и** serve to show hardness or softness of the previous consonant while representing the same vowel sound.

The **ь** is used to indicate the softness of a consonant if there is no vowel following it: брат**ь**, угол**ь**.

а	о	у	э	ы		indicate that the preceding consonant is **hard**
|	|	|	|	|		
я	ё	ю	е	и	ь	indicate that the preceding consonant is **soft**

The hushing sounds represented by letters **Ч ч**, **Щщ**, **Ж ж**, **Ш ш** as well as the letters **Ц ц** and **Й й** do not form hard and soft pairs. **Ч ч**, **Щ щ** and **Й й** are considered to be soft by nature while **Ж ж**, **Ш ш**, **Ц ц** are always hard.

> **Spelling Clues**
> Remember that **Ч ч**, **Щ щ**, **Ж ж**, **Ш ш**, **Ц ц** are usually (with very few exceptions) followed by vowels **а**, **о**, **у** and **е**, **и**.
> The letter **Ц ц** is followed by **и** in the middle and by **ы** at the end of a word (**ци**рк, but кана́д**цы**).
> **Й й** appears at the very end of a word or if followed by another consonant (ча**й**, ча́**й**ник). In a rare occasion it appears at the beginning of a loan word like **йо́**гурт or **йо́**га.

1.4–2. Слу́шайте и повторя́йте. Focus on the proper pronunciation of hard and soft consonants.

ма́сло — мя́со		мэр — ме́ра		живо́т — живёт		му́зыка — мю́зикл	
butter	*meat*	*mayor*	*measure*	*stomach*	*he/she lives*	*music*	*musical show*

быть — бить		мел — мель		То́ма —	Тёма —	те́ма	да — дя́дя	
to be	*to beat*	*chalk*	*sandbar*	*Toma girl's name*	*Tyoma boy's name*	*topic, theme*	*yes*	*uncle*

Мя́гкий знак — Soft sign

ь

- Shows that the preceding consonant is soft when there is no vowel after the consonant. It can even distinguish words (**брат** and **брать**, **мел** and **мель**);
- Indicates where **е**, **ё**, **ю**, **я** represent two sounds **ye**, **yo**, **yu**, **ya** (like in **статья́** — *article*) after a soft consonant.

Твёрдый знак — Hard sign

ъ

- Indicates where **е**, **ё**, **ю**, **я** represent two sounds **ye**, **yo**, **yu**, **ya** but the consonant is hard (and therefore the ь cannot be used) (like in **объе́кт** — *object*);
- Rarely used in contemporary Russian.

1.4–3. **Слу́шайте и повторя́йте.**

ию́нь	ию́ль	янва́рь	слова́рь	жизнь	апельси́н
June	*July*	*January*	*dictionary*	*life*	*orange*
сел	съел	объе́кт	объём	объе́хал	
he sat down	*he ate up*	*object*	*volume, capacity*	*he drove around*	

Vowel Reduction: Letters о, а, е, я

You already know that the letter **o** is reduced when not stressed. You have probably noticed that the letter **a** is also reduced in unstressed positions. The following chart summarizes vowel reduction rules for **o** and **a**.

о, а → [**a**] Immediately before the stressed syllable, this ***a**-sound* is weaker than the stressed **a**.

о, а → [**ə**] In other unstressed positions, this sound is close to ***a*** in ***a**bove*.

1.4–4. **Слу́шайте и повторя́йте.**

[**a**] before the stressed syllable

стака́н	бана́н	окно́	дома́	очки́	слова́

[**ə**] in other unstressed positions

ма́ма	па́па	ча́шка	ма́сло	кни́га	я́блоко	до́ма

1.4–5. **Слу́шайте и повторя́йте.** Listen and repeat these familiar three-syllable words. Note the pronunciation of o and a in different positions.

Write	Say
соба́ка	саба́кə
доро́га	даро́гə
маши́на	маши́нə
хорошо́	хəрашо́
молоко́	мəлако́
каранда́ш	кəранда́ш

доро́га — *road*

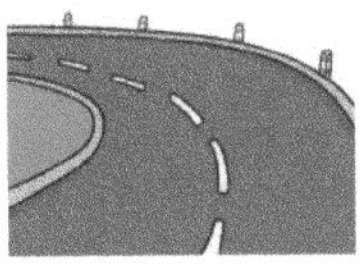

Two other letters also undergo reduction in unstressed positions: е and я.

е, я → [**и**] before the stressed syllable

е, я → [**уə**] after the stressed syllable

1.4–6. Слу́шайте и повторя́йте.

[и] before the stressed syllable

Write	Say	Translation
телефо́н	тил**и**фо́н	*telephone*
сестра́	с**и**стра́	*sister*
лягу́шка	л**и**гу́шка	*frog*
в октябре́	в **ə**кт**и**бре́	*in October*

The further the sound is from the stressed syllable the more it is reduced. If you listen carefully, you will hear that the first **и**-sound in **телефо́н** is weaker than the **и**-sound in the second syllable.

1.4–7. Слу́шайте и повторя́йте.

[уə] at end of a word (**у** symbol here shows the softness of the preceding consonant)

Write	Say	Translation
Росси́я	Расси**уə**	*Russia*
Англия	Англи**уə**	*England*
дя́дя	дя́д**уə**	*uncle*
тётя	тёт**уə**	*aunt*
скажи́те	скажи́т**уə**	*tell me (plural)*
пиши́те	пиши́т**уə**	*write (plural)*
учи́тель	учи́т**уəль**	teacher

Numerals 1-12

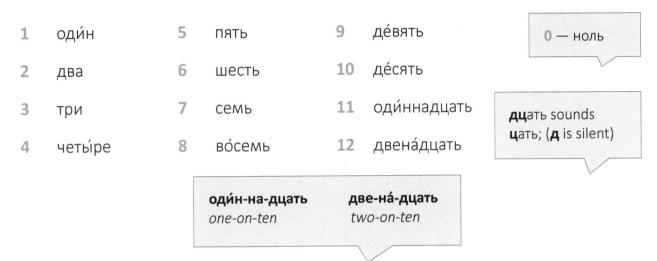

1.4–8. Слу́шайте и повторя́йте. Pay attention to the vowel reductions in the numerals.

1	оди́н	5	пять	9	де́вять
2	два	6	шесть	10	де́сять
3	три	7	семь	11	оди́ннадцать
4	четы́ре	8	во́семь	12	двена́дцать

0 — ноль

дцать sounds **ц**ать; (**д** is silent)

оди́н-на-дцать *one-on-ten*

две-на́-дцать *two-on-ten*

1.4–9. Answer the questions with one word (the number) in Russian.

Образе́ц. Model: How many courses are you taking this term? — Три.

1. How many cities have you lived in?
2. How many foreign cities have you visited?
3. How many cities have you visited in your country?
4. How many Russian classes do you have per week?
5. How many hours per week do you do your Russian homework?
6. How many hours do you sleep a night?
7. How many legs do insects have?
8. How many vowels are in the Russian alphabet?
9. How many Russian authors have you heard of? Which ones?
10. List all numbers not mentioned in previous answers.

Поговори́м!

1.4–10. In groups of 5-6 people, play a game which Russians call **Сло́манный телефо́н** — *'A broken phone'*.

Your teacher will whisper a four digit number in such a way that only one player in your group can hear it. The person who now knows the number whispers it in the ear of the next player in his/her team, and so on until the number reaches the ear of the last player. When all teams have finished whispering, the last player from each team should say the number out loud. The team that gets the right number wins the game. For a more challenging game, try five and more digit numbers.

Formal and Informal Conversations

The level of formality determines how Russians would introduce themselves. Adults normally introduce themselves and greet each other formally when they first meet. Children and teenagers introduce themselves and greet each other informally.

To reflect this, Russian has two words for *you*: **ты** and **вы**.

you

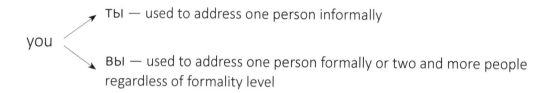

- ты — used to address one person informally
- вы — used to address one person formally or two and more people regardless of formality level

The pronouns **ты** and **вы** can change their form. You will learn later how they change and why. For now, you should be able to recognize **тебя́** as a form of **ты** and **вас** as a form of **вы**.

Greetings and Goodbyes

1.4–11. Слу́шайте и повторя́йте.

Formal	Informal	Translation
Здра́вствуйте!	Приве́т!	*Hello! Hi!*
Как вас зову́т?	Как тебя́ зову́т?	*What is your name?*
Отку́да вы?	Отку́да ты?	*Where are you from?*
До свида́ния!	Пока́!	*Good bye! Bye!*

Other common greetings and goodbyes can be used both formally and informally:

1.4–12. Слу́шайте и повторя́йте.

До́брое у́тро!	*Good morning!*
До́брый день!	*Good afternoon!*
До́брый ве́чер!	*Good evening!*
До за́втра!	*See you tomorrow! (Literally: "Till tomorrow")*
До встре́чи!	*See you! (Literally: "Until we meet")*
Споко́йной но́чи!	*Good night! Night-night!*

вт sounds **фт**
вс sounds **фс**

Being Polite

Being polite is important everywhere. Start using these words and expressions with your teacher and classmates today!

1.4–13. Слу́шайте и повторя́йте.

Спаси́бо!	*Thank you!*
Пожа́луйста!	*1) You are welcome! 2) Please. 3) There you go!*
Извини́те.	*1) Excuse me / Pardon me. 2) I'm sorry.*
Скажи́те, пожа́луйста!	*Tell me please... or: Could you tell me...*

Asking for Additional Information: ИК-4

ИК-4 is used for questions beginning with **А** that ask for additional information. The English equivalent is "And how about...?" The tone falls on the centre of the **ИК** and rises at the post-central part. If there is no post-central part, the tone rises and then falls slightly on the centre.

— —___ /　　　___ /　　　**ИК-4**

А Ната́ша?　　　А вы?

1.4–14. Слу́шайте и повторя́йте.

Меня́ зову́т Макс[1]. А как вас[4] зову́т?	*My name is Max. And what's your name?*
Меня́ зову́т Лена[1]. А тебя[4]?	*My name is Lena. And yours?*
Я из Англии[1]. А вы[4]?	*I'm from England? And (how about) you?*
Я студент[1]. А ты[4]?	*I'm a student. And (how about) you?*
Ма́ма дома[1]. — А папа[4]?	*Mom is at home. — And (how about) dad?*

1.4–15. Слу́шайте и чита́йте диало́г. Listen to and read the dialogue.

Pay attention to the intonation on the **ИК-4** questions.

— До́брый день!

Good afternoon!

— Здра́вствуйте. Меня́ зову́т Татья́на. А как вас[4] зову́т?

Hello. My name is Tatyana. And what's your name?

— Меня́ зову́т Пётр. Прия́тно познако́ми**ться**.

My name is Peter. Nice to meet you.

— Очень прия́тно! Пётр, вы студе́нт?

Nice to meet you! Peter, are you a student?

— Да, я студе́нт. А вы[4]?

Yes, I'm a student. And you?

— Я учи́тель.

I'm a teacher.

— Пра́вда?

Really?

— Да. Я то́лько начала́ рабо́тать.

Yes. I just started working.

— Очень интере́сно!

Very interesting!

> **ться** and **тся** combinations are pronounced as if they were spelled **ца.**
>
> **Очень прия́тно** literally means: *"Very pleased".*

1.4–16. Слу́шайте и чита́йте диало́г. Pay attention to the intonation on the ИК-4 questions.

— Приве́т!

Hi!

— Приве́т! Меня́ зову́т Макси́м. А как тебя́[4] зову́т?

Hi! My name is Maxim. And what's your name?

он — студе́нт
она́ — студе́нтка

— Меня́ зову́т Са́ра. Я из Кана́ды. А отку́да ты[4]?

My name is Sara. I'm from Canada. Where are you from?

— Из Росси́и. Я студе́нт. Учу́сь здесь в Ло́ндоне. А ты[4]?

From Russia. I'm a student. I study here in London. How about you?

— Я то́же студе́нтка.

I'm a student too.

— Прия́тно познако́миться, Са́ра!

Nice to meet you Sara!

— Очень прия́тно!

Nice to meet you!

1.4–17. Formal or informal? Which of the two dialogues above is the example of formal speech situation and which one is informal? Find the clue words that support your choice of formal and informal.

Поговори́м!

1.4–18. Introduce yourself to a classmate; say that you are a student; and tell your classmate where you from and where you study (ask your teacher to help you with the endings for places). Ask your partner similar questions. Use dialogues from the exercises above as a model.

Russian Names: и́мя, о́тчество, фами́лия

Russians have three names: first name — **и́мя**, patronymic — **о́тчество**, and last name — **фами́лия**.

- **Имя** is a name given to a new born baby by his or her parents. Normally, there is only one given name and no second (middle) name.

  Russians are fond of using numerous variations of **и́мя**. Suffixes are used for friendly, informal and affectionate versions of **и́мя**. In official papers they have the full form of a given name: **Екатери́на**, **Мари́я**, **Татья́на**, **Ива́н**, **Михаи́л**. People, however, would most likely be called different in different situations. Below are some examples of names variations:

Formal	Informal (Neutral)	Affectionate
Екатери́на	Ка́тя	Ка́тенька, Катю́ша
Мари́я	Ма́ша	Ма́шенька, Машу́тка
Татья́на	Та́ня	Та́нечка, Таню́ша
Ива́н	Ва́ня	Ва́нечка, Ваню́ша
Михаи́л	Ми́ша	Ми́шенька, Мишу́тка
Серге́й	Серёжа	Серёженька

- **Отчество** is the first name of the person's father with a suffix added to it: **-ович (-евич)** for a male person and **-овна (-евна)** for a female. Thus, if a boy's father's first name is **Иван**, that boy's **о́тчество** is **Ива́нович**. If the girl's father's name is **Ива́н**, her **о́тчество** is **Ива́новна**.

  The patronymic names always follow the formal version of one's first name: **Михаи́л Ива́нович**, **Екатери́на Ива́новна**. Such combination **и́мя + о́тчество** is used in formal situations. All children, for example, address their teachers at school by their first and patronymic names. Since the **и́мя + о́тчество** reserved for formal situations, it is inappropriate to combine informal or affectionate versions of one's first name (like **Ка́тя, Ка́тенька**) with his or her patronymic name.

- **Фами́лия** — a child's last name is traditionally inherited from his or her father (a single mom may give her own last name to her child). The Russian last name for a female slightly differs from that of a male: a feminine gender ending (**-а**, **-ая**) will be added to the last name. Compare: **Пу́шкин** and **Пу́шкина**, **Горбачёв** and **Горбачёва**, **Толсто́й** and **Толста́я**.

  Note that the last name does not always come last. On lists of names, it stays first. In formal introductions, it can be mentioned first or last like in the formal dialogue below.

1.4–19. Чита́йте диало́г. Read the dialogue with a partner.

— Меня́ зову́т Анна Серге́евна Мо́нина.

— Петро́в Алекса́ндр Никола́евич. Очень рад познако́миться.

— Очень прия́тно.

1.4–20. А. Чита́йте. Read the full names of famous Russians and the brief descriptions of who they were.

Алекса́ндр Серге́евич Пу́шкин
(поэ́т, оте́ц ру́сской литерату́ры)

Лев Никола́евич Толсто́й
(писа́тель, фило́соф)

Фёдор Миха́йлович Достое́вский
(оте́ц психологи́ческого рома́на)

Анна Андре́евна Ахма́това
(поэ́т, литерату́рный кри́тик)

Мари́на Ива́новна Цвета́ева
(поэ́т, проза́ик)

Анто́н Па́влович Че́хов
(писа́тель, драмату́рг, врач)

Михаил Серге́евич Горбачёв
(президе́нт СССР)

Юрий Алексе́евич Гага́рин
(пе́рвый челове́к в ко́смосе)

Раиса Макси́мовна Горбачёва
(жена́ президе́нта СССР)

Поговори́м!

1.4–21. Just for fun. Imagine you are one of the persons above. With a partner, introduce yourselves formally as famous Russians. Remember to use first, patronymic, and last names for your formal introduction.

Урок 5

Voiced and Voiceless Consonants

Like English, Russian has voiced and voiceless consonants. If you put your fingers on your throat while making a sound "z-z-z-z-z-z-z...," you will feel your vocal cords vibrating. If you do the same thing while producing a sound "s-s-s-s-s-s-s...," you will notice that your vocal cords remain still.

Keep your fingers on your throat and say the English words "zoo" — "sue", "zip" — "sip". Notice the difference in voicing between the words in each pair.

The z- sound is voiced and s-sound is voiceless. Russian voiced and voiceless consonants are listed below in pairs. Except for voicing, each pair has identical articulation.

1.5–1. Слу́шайте и повторя́йте. Keep your fingers on your throat while pronouncing these sounds and words. Notice the voicing differences between the pairs of sounds.

Voiced	в	б	д	ж	з	г
Voiceless	ф	п	т	ш	с	к

бар — пар	*bar — steam*	жар — шар	*heat — balloon*
ва́за — фа́за	*vase — phase*	зуб — суп	*tooth — soup*
до́чка — то́чка	*daughter — point, dot*	год — кот	*year — cat*

Final Consonant Devoicing

At the end of **зуб**, you hear [**п**] and at the end of **год** — [**т**]. This is called **final consonant devoicing**. When there is a voiced consonant at the very end of the word, it is pronounced as its voiceless counterpart.

1.5–2. Слу́шайте и повторя́йте. Pay attention to the very last sound in each word.

зуб — суп	*tooth — soup*	снег — челове́к	*snow — person*
год — кот	*year — cat*	род — рот	*gender, kin — mouth*
глаз — класс	*eye — class*		

1.5–3. Слу́шайте и повторя́йте. Remember that final consonants must be devoiced.

Че́хов	друг	джаз	го́род	нож	лоб
Chekhov	*friend*	*jazz*	*city*	*knife*	*forehead*

Voiced-Voiceless Assimilation

When a voiced and a voiceless consonant stay together, they assimilate: the nature of the second consonant determines how the first one must be pronounced. For example, in the word **ска́зка** — *fairy tale* we hear [**ск**] in the middle because the second consonant **к** is voiceless, and it forces the first consonant to become voiceless, too. Conversely, in the word **футбо́л** — *soccer* we hear [**дб**] in the middle. Here, the second consonant **б** is voiced, and it changes the **т** to a **д** sound.

1.5–4. Слу́шайте и повторя́йте. Remember to devoice all the final voiced consonants.

voiced + voiceless → voiceless cluster

ска́зка [ск]	оши́бка [пк]	ло́жка [шк]	субти́тры [пт]
fairy tale	*mistake*	*spoon*	*subtitles*
за́втра [фт]	вчера́ [фч]	вход [вх]	авто́бус [фт]
tomorrow	*yesterday*	*entrance*	*bus*

voiceless + voiced → voiced cluster

футбо́л [дб]	вокза́л [гз]	спортза́л [дз]	сда́ча [зд]
soccer	*train station*	*gym*	*change*
та́кже [гж]	рюкза́к [гз]		
also	*backpack*		

Letters **в, л, м, н, р** do not affect pronunciation of the preceding consonant. For example, in the word **ма́сло** – *butter* we hear [**сл**] in the middle and in **фру́кты** – *fruit* we hear [**фр**].

voiceless + в, л, м, н, р → the first consonant remains voiceless

бу́ква [кв]	ма́сло [сл]	приве́т [пр]	Смотри́! [см] [тр]
letter	*butter*	*hi*	*Look!*

Consonant assimilation is not limited to a cluster within a single word. It occurs between words too.

1.5–5. Слу́шайте и повторя́йте. Remember to devoice all the final voiced consonants.

Как вас зову́т? [зз]	Я из Кана́ды. [ск]	Как дела́? [гд]
What's your name?	*I'm from Canada.*	*How are you?*
Как жизнь? [гж]	Всё [фс] в поря́дке. [фп]	
How is life?	*Everything is all right. (Literally: "in order")*	

Final consonant devoicing and **consonant assimilation** rules apply to both hard and soft consonants. In rare occasions, both rules can apply within one cluster (like in **дождь** and **гвоздь**). In this case, final devoicing rule comes first and the whole cluster sounds voiceless.

1.5–6. Слу́шайте и повторя́йте. Explain the difference between the pronunciation and spelling.

любо́вь	це́рковь	дождь	по́езд	гвоздь
love	*church*	*rain*	*train*	*nail*

1.5–7. А. Слу́шайте и повторя́йте. Listen and repeat. Focus on the pronunciation of difficult consonant clusters. Read the syllables first, then read the words.

фтра, фтрак, фся, афся, хле, хлеп
сла, сли, фки, гже, фку, сна, шка

Say	Write	Translation
за́-фтрак	за́втрак	*breakfast*
афся́-на-я	овся́ная	*made of oats*
ма́-сла	ма́сло	*butter*
сли́-фки	сли́вки	*cream*
фку́-сна	вку́сно	*tasty*
ло́-шка	ло́жка	*spoon*

Б. Чита́йте. Read. Remember about vowel reduction (**о**, **а**, **е**, **я**), final consonant devoicing and consonant assimilation.

Это мой за́втрак. Вот овся́ная ка́ша, хлеб, ма́сло, сыр. Там ко́фе, молоко́, сли́вки, а та́кже мёд. Всё о́чень вку́сно! А где ло́жка и нож?

This is my breakfast. Here is oatmeal, bread, butter, cheese. There is coffee, milk, cream, and also honey. Everything is very tasty! And where is spoon and knife?

В. In the text above find the examples of vowel reduction, final consonant devoicing, and consonant assimilation.

Поговори́м!

1.5–8. Pretend that you can't remember some Russian words. Ask your partner the "wrong" question about the items below. Your partner should correct you, and say the proper Russian word for each item. Take turns reading the questions and answering them.

Образец:

— Это апельси́н?
— Нет, э́то не апельси́н. Это я́блоко.

— Это вокза́л?

— Это ло́жка?

— Это дом?

— Это борщ?

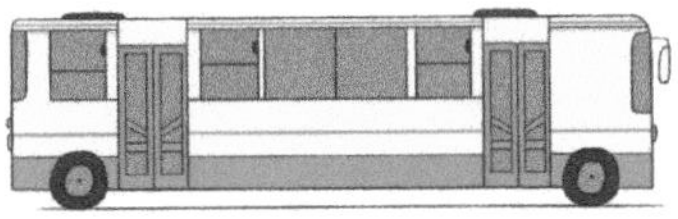

— Это по́езд?

— Это ча́шка?

1.5–9. Игра́ем в слова́. Word play. Sort these breakfast items by categories.

Апельси́н, бана́н, ви́лка, вода́, йо́гурт, ко́фе, лимо́н, ло́жка, ма́сло, мёд, молоко́, нож, овся́ная ка́ша, сли́вки, сок, стака́н, сыр, таре́лка, тост, хлеб, чай, ча́йник, ча́шка, шокола́д, я́блоко.

ви́лка — *fork*
таре́лка — *plate*

Посу́да — *Utensils*

Напи́тки — *Drinks*

Фру́кты — *Fruits*

Сла́дости — *Sweets*

Друга́я еда́ — *Other foods*

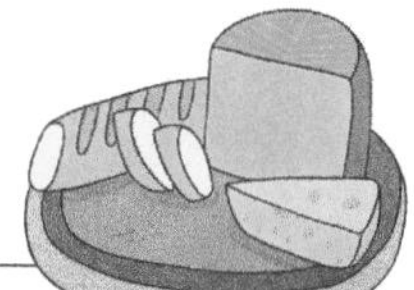

Поговори́м!

1.5–10. Мой за́втрак. Make a quick drawing of your breakfast, and explain to your partner what you eat for breakfast by pointing to the items on your drawing and naming them. The text and vocabulary from previous exercises will help you to create the conversation. Your partner should ask about something that is missing on your picture: А где...? Add the item your partner asked about to the drawing and say: Вот он (она, оно). Remember that the pronoun you must use (он, она, оно) depends on the gender of the noun.

- **Когда́? — When?**

1.5–11. Слу́шайте и повторя́йте. Pay attention to vowel reduction.

Когда́?

у́тром	днём	ве́чером	но́чью

- **Во ско́лько? — At what time?**

1.5–12. Слу́шайте и повторя́йте. Be sure to have the proper vowel reduction, consonant assimilation and final consonant devoicing for each word.

Во ско́лько?

В час.	В пять часо́в.	В де́вять часо́в.
В два часа́.	В шесть часо́в.	В де́сять часо́в.
В три часа́.	В семь часо́в.	В оди́ннадцать часо́в.
В четы́ре часа́.	В во́семь часо́в.	В двена́дцать часо́в.

1.5–13. Когда́? Во ско́лько? In Russian, provide short answers for the questions below. Your answers should be approximate, as you have not learned how to say time in minutes yet.

Образе́ц: When do you get home after classes? What time? — Ве́чером. В пять часо́в.

1. When do you wake up? What time?
2. When do you have breakfast? What time?
3. When do you go to classes? What time?
4. When do you have lunch? What time?
5. When do you go to the library? What time?
6. When do you have dinner? What time?
7. When do you go for a walk? What time?
8. When do you to the movies? What time?
9. When do you do homework? What time?
10. When do you go to sleep? What time?

1.5–14. А. Слу́шайте и повторя́йте. Be sure to have the proper vowel reduction, consonant assimilation and final consonant devoicing for each word.

сю, сюр, прис, фсё, фпа, ря, тки, тли, чна
слу, шай, фтра, што, жна, фстре, ти, ца, ка, не, шна

Say	Write	Translation
сюр-при́с	сюрпри́з	*surprise*
фсё-фпа-ря́-тки	всё в поря́дке	*everything is all right*
фсё-а-тли́-чна	всё отли́чно	*everything is great*
фстре́-ти-ца	встре́титься	*to meet*
ка-не́-шна	коне́чно	*sure*
да-фстре́-чи	до встре́чи	*until we meet (see you)*
да-за́-фтра	до за́втра	*see you tomorrow*

Б. Слу́шайте и чита́йте диало́г. Don't forget about final consonant devoicing and consonant assimilation.

— Аня, приве́т! Како́й сюрпри́з!

Anya, hi! What a surprise!

— Приве́т, Оле́г! Как жизнь?

Hi Oleg! How is life?

встре́титься — *to meet with* is pronounced [**ф**стре́ти**ца**]

— Всё в поря́дке. А как ты?

Everything is all right. And how are you?

— У меня́ всё отли́чно. Слу́шай, ты за́втра до́ма?

I'm doing great. Listen, are you home tomorrow?

коне́чно — *of course* is pronounced [к**а**не́**шнə**]

— Да, а что?

Yes. Why?

— Ну́жно встре́титься. У меня́ есть для тебя́ рабо́та.

We need to meet. I have a job for you.

— Хорошо́. Не пробле́ма. Когда́?

Okay. No problem. When?

— Мо́жно у́тром?

Can we meet in the morning?

— Да, коне́чно. Утром я до́ма. Приходи́ в де́сять часо́в.

Yes, sure. I'm home in the morning. Come over at 10 o'clock.

— Спаси́бо! Тогда́ до встре́чи.

Thank you! See you then.

— До за́втра.

See you tomorrow.

В. In the dialogue above, find the examples of

— vowel reduction;

— final consonant devoicing;

— consonant assimilation.

1.5–15. Как по-ру́сски? How would you say this in Russian?

1. What a surprise!
2. How are you?
3. I'm doing great.
4. Are you home tomorrow?
5. We need to meet.
6. I'm home in the morning.
7. Come over.
8. See you tomorrow.
9. See you then.
10. Of course.

Поговори́м!

1.5–16. Ну́жно встре́титься. We need to meet.

А. With a partner, create a mini-dialogue to arrange for a meeting. Follow the model replacing phrases in bold with your own.

Образе́ц:

А) — Ну́жно встре́титься.

Б) — Не пробле́ма. Когда́?

А) **— За́втра ве́чером. В шесть часо́в.**

Б) **— А мо́жно в семь?**

А) — Да, коне́чно.

Б) — Хорошо́. Тогда́ до встре́чи.

А) **— Пока́!**

Б. With a partner, create a longer conversation. Imagine you run into a friend you need to see. You have a book for your friend. Arrange for a meeting at home in the evening at a certain time. Use phrases from the dialogues above as construction blocks for your conversation.

Урок 6

Counting in Russian

If you know numerals from 1-12, it should be easy for you to learn counting. Review your first twelve Russian numerals before you go further (refer to Урóк 4).

Read the following numbers aloud: 10, 9, 1, 11, 2, 12, 7, 8, 6, 5, 4, 3.

Посчитáем! Let's count!

1.6–1. А. Working with a partner, formulate and solve easy math problems. Follow the model given below in the Образéц. Take turns asking and answering the questions.

Образéц:	— Скóлько бýдет два плюс два?	— *How much will be two plus two?*
	— Четы́ре.	— *Four.*
	— Скóлько бýдет четы́ре ми́нус оди́н?	— *How much will be four minus one?*
	— Три.	— *Three.*

1) 1 + 3 = ...	3) 7 – 3 = ...	5) 11 – 6 = ...	7) 9 – 4 = ...
2) 5 + 2 = ...	4) 10 – 4 = ...	6) 8 + 4 = ...	8) 12 – 9 = ...

Б. Formulate two problems of your own. Ask you partner to solve them.

Numerals 11-19

Memorize the numerals 11–19. Read the *Notes* below to learn how these numerals are related to the ones you already know.

1.6–2. Слу́шайте и повторя́йте. Pay attention to vowel reduction in the numerals.

11	оди́ннадцать	один + на + дцать
12	двена́дцать	две + на + дцать
13	трина́дцать	три + на + дцать
14	четы́рнадцать	четыр + на + дцать
15	пятна́дцать	пят + на + дцать
16	шестна́дцать	шест + на + дцать
17	семна́дцать	сем + на + дцать
18	восемна́дцать	восем + на + дцать
19	девятна́дцать	девят + на + дцать

Notes

- All *"teens"* have **надцать** component where **на** means *"on"* and **дцать** means ***"ten"***, so you read them as *"one on ten"*, *"two on ten"*, etc.
- In 12, **два** changes to **две**.
- Numerals 15-19 have no central **ь**
- all "teens" have final **ь**.
- **Дц**ать sounds [**ц**]ать (**д** is silent).

Numerals 20 - 100

Memorize the numerals 20 – 100. Read the *Notes* to learn how they are formed.

1.6–3. Слу́шайте и повторя́йте. Pay attention to vowel reduction.

20	два́дцать	два + дцать
30	три́дцать	три + дцать
40	со́рок	сорок
50	пятьдеся́т	пять + десят
60	шестьдеся́т	шесть + десят
70	се́мьдесят	семь + десят
80	во́семьдесят	восемь + десят
90	девяно́сто	девя+но+сто
100	сто	сто

Notes

- Numerals 20-90 do not have the **на** component in the middle.
- **Дцать** is used for ***"ten"*** in 20 and 30; you read them as *"two tens"*, *"three tens"*.
- **Десят** is used for ***"ten"*** in 50-80; there is no **ь** at the end but there is one in the middle.
- Historically, 40 and 90 are formed in a different way.

Compound numerals

Compound numerals are formed by placing simple numerals in sequence: два́дцать оди́н — 21, три́дцать два — 32, сто двена́дцать — 112, сто три́дцать четы́ре — 134. Read the examples of compound numerals below:

1.6–4. Слу́шайте и повторя́йте. Pay attention to vowel reduction.

21	два́дцать оди́н
32	три́дцать два
43	со́рок три
54	пятьдеся́т четы́ре
65	шестьдеся́т пять
99	девяно́сто девя́ть
101	сто оди́н
111	сто оди́ннадцать
178	сто се́мьдесят во́семь

Notes

- Write compound numerals as separate words, without hyphens.

Memorize phrases that your instructor will be using regularly in class.

1.6–5. Слу́шайте учи́теля и повторя́йте. Listen to your teacher read the phrases and repeat the phrases.

1.	Откро́йте учё́бники на страни́це два́дцать оди́н.	*Open your textbooks on page 21.*
2.	Упражне́ние пять на страни́це два́дцать во́семь.	*Exercise 5 on page 28.*
3.	Откро́йте тетра́ди на страни́це семна́дцать.	*Open your exercise books on page 17.*

1.6–6. Read the following numbers out loud.

107, 110, 113, 124, 135, 146, 158, 169, 170, 181, 192

Review of Intonation Contours: ИК-1, ИК-2, ИК-3, and ИК-4

1.6-7. В классе. *In the classroom*. Read the questions and statements below. Remember to use proper intonation: **ИК-1** in simple statements, **ИК-2** in questions with question words, and **ИК-3** in yes-no questions.

Это стул.

Это компьютер?

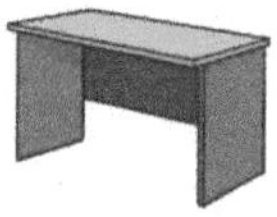

Это стол.

Это проектор?

– Где ру́чка? – Вот она́.

– А каранда́ш? – Вот он.

– Это кни́га? – Да, это кни́га.

– Вот кни́га, бума́га, каранда́ш и ру́чка.

– А э́то? – Это слова́рь.

– Где окно́?
– Вот оно́.

– Это твой рюкза́к?
– Да, мой.

– Это слова́рь?
– Нет, э́то тетра́дь.

– Что э́то?
– Это учё́бник.

Поговорим! Let's talk!

1.6-8. A. Working with a partner, talk about things in a typical classroom. Ask at least

- three questions with the question word **Где**...?;
- three questions with the question words **Кто** ...? or **Что** ...?;
- three yes-no questions;
- two questions asking for additional information: **А это**?

Образе́ц: – Где прое́ктор? – Вот он.
– Что э́то? – Это прое́ктор.
– А э́то? – Это компью́тер.
– Это прое́ктор? – Да, э́то прое́ктор.

учи́тель – *primary, grade school teacher*

преподава́тель – *university, college teacher*

Point to the items on the picture below and use the following vocabulary: студе́нт, студе́нтка, преподава́тель, доска́ (*chalkboard*), коло́нки (*speakers*), стол, стул, компью́тер, бума́га, кни́га, каранда́ш, ру́чка, учё́бник, тетра́дь, окно́, ва́за, мел, бу́ква «Я», ка́ктус. Take turns asking and answering question.

Б. Working with a different partner, talk about things in your classroom. Ask **Где...? Кто...? Что...? А это?** and yes-no questions. Remember to use proper intonation contours.

Чита́ем и понима́ем. Reading Russian tongue twisters and poems

This section provides you with authentic Russian texts: tongue twisters, proverbs, poems, stories, and folk tales accompanied by translation, comments, questions, and assignments. They are also recorded for you to listen. Read the tongue twisters and little poems aloud. You may choose to listen to the recordings first. (You will find the recordings on this chapter webpage.)

Remember the reading rules you have learned: vowel reduction of unstressed syllables, consonant assimilation and final consonant devoicing. Each poem focuses on a certain sound. Try to articulate that sound as clearly as you can.

Sounds ы — и

Если ру́ки мы́ли мы,	*If we washed hands,*
Если ру́ки мы́ли вы,	*If you, guys, washed hands,*
Если ру́ки мыл и ты,	*And if you, my friend, washed hands,*
Зна́чит ру́ки вы́мыты!	*That means hands are clean!*

п and unstressed о

Попуга́й говори́т попуга́ю:	*A parrot says to a parrot:*
— Попуга́й, я тебя́ попуга́ю.	*— Parrot, I'm going to startle you.*
Отвеча́ет ему́ попуга́й:	*The parrot answers to the parrot:*
— Попуга́й, попуга́й, попуга́й!	*— Startle, startle, startle!*

Rolling р — р' and unstressed о

Коро́ль — орёл!	*The king is an eagle!*
Орёл — коро́ль!	*An eagle is the king!*

— Расскажи́те про поку́пки.	*Tell me about things you've bought.*
— Про каки́е про поку́пки?	*What kind of things?*
— Про поку́пки, про поку́пки,	*About things, about things,*
Про поку́почки свои́.	*About all the little things you've bought.*

Два́дцать пять профессоро́в	*Twenty five professors*
Изуча́ли комаро́в	*Were studying mosquitos*
И проси́ли комаро́в	*And they asked mosquitos*
Не куса́ть профессоро́в.	*Not to bite the professors.*

(П. Синявский)

Зада́ние 1. In the tongue twisters you have read, find and read aloud examples of:

a) words with unstressed, and therefore reduced, vowels о, е, and я and
b) words with devoiced final consonants.

Зада́ние 2. Memorize two tongue twisters and say them to your classmates.

Акти́вный слова́рь. Те́ма 1

Question Words

где — *where*

как — *how*

когда́ — *when*

кто — *who*

отку́да — *where from*

что — *what*

Nouns
Кто? Что?

бу́ква — *letter* (*character*)

вопро́с — *question*

дом — *house*

друг (pl. друзья́) — *friend*

каранда́ш — *pencil*

оши́бка — *mistake*

сло́во — *word*

студе́нт — *student* (*male*)

студе́нтка — *student* (*female*)

рабо́та — *work*

ру́чка — *pen*

учи́тель — *teacher*

Parts of the Day
Когда́?

у́тром — *in the morning*

днём — *in the afternoon, in the daytime*

ве́чером — *in the evening*

но́чью — *at night*

Фра́зы — Phrases

Во ско́лько? — *At what time?*

Всё в поря́дке! — *Everything is all right!*

До встре́чи! — *See you! Until we meet!*

До за́втра! — *See you tomorrow!*

До свида́ния! — *Goodbye!*

До́брое у́тро! — *Good morning!*

До́брый ве́чер! — *Good evening!*

До́брый день! — *Good afternoon!*

Здра́вствуйте! — *Hello!*

Извини́те. — *Excuse me.*

Как дела́? — *How are you?*

Как жизнь? — *How is life?*

Коне́чно! — *Of course!*

Ну́жно встре́титься. — *We have to meet.*

Отли́чно! — *Excellent!*

Очень прия́тно! — *Very pleased!*

Пожа́луйста! — *1) You are welcome!; 2) please*

Пока́! — *Bye!*

Приве́т! — *Hi!*

Прия́тно познако́миться — *It's a pleasure to meet you!*

Спаси́бо! — *Thank you!*

Споко́йной но́чи! — *Good night!*

Тема 2
Кто вы? Откуда вы?

Практика

- **Отку́да вы?** Where are you from?
- **Профе́ссии.** Talking about professions and occupations
- **Я говорю́ по-ру́сски.** Discussing language skills

Грамматика

- Grammatical gender of nouns
- Russian verbs. The present tense. Introduction
- Question **Как?** *How?* Adverbs
- The verb **писа́ть** — *to write*
- Russian verbs. Past tense

Культура

- Professions and gender

Читаем и понимаем

- Reading Russian folk tale **"Ку́рочка Ря́ба"** *Riaba the Hen*

Акти́вный слова́рь. Те́ма 2

Nouns
Профе́ссии — Professions, Occupations
Кто?

актёр — *actor*

актри́са — *actress*

аспира́нт — *graduate student (male)*

аспира́нтка — *graduate student (female)*

балери́на — *ballerina*

бизнесме́н — *businessman*

врач — *doctor*

гимна́ст — *gymnast (male)*

гимна́стка — *gymnast (female)*

журнали́ст — *journalist*

журнали́стка — *journalist (female)*

инжене́р — *engineer*

компози́тор — *composer*

космона́вт — *astronaut, cosmonaut*

мини́стр — *minister*

музыка́нт — *musician*

пе́вец — *singer (male)*

певи́ца — *singer (female)*

перево́дчик — *translator*

писа́тель — *writer*

писа́тельница — *writer (female)*

президе́нт — *president*

преподава́тель — *instructor, professor*

преподава́тельница — *instructor, professor (female)*

продаве́ц — *shop assistant*

продавщи́ца — *shop assistant (female)*

спортсме́н — *athlete*

спортсме́нка — *athlete (female)*

танцо́р — *dancer*

теннеси́ст — *tennis player (male)*

теннеси́стка — *tennis player (female)*

фигури́ст — *figure skater (male)*

фигури́стка — *figure skater (female)*

шко́льник — *schoolboy*

шко́льница — *schoolgirl*

юри́ст — *lawyer*

Семья́ — Family
Кто?

ба́бушка — *grandmother, grandma, granny*

де́душка — *grandfather, grandpa*

ма́ма — *mom*

па́па — *dad*

муж — *husband*

жена́ — *wife*

брат — *brother*

сестра́ — *sister*

дя́дя — *uncle*

тётя — *aunt*

сын — *son*

до́чка — *daughter (diminutive)*

дочь — *daughter(female)*

Other nouns
Что?

газе́та — *newspaper*

диало́г — *dialogue*

журна́л — *journal; magazine*

календа́рь — *calendar (male)*

музе́й — *museum*

образе́ц — *model, sample*

отве́т — *answer*

перево́д — *translation*

письмо́ — *letter*

пра́вило — *rule*

расска́з — *story*

страни́ца — *page*

текст — *text*

тест — *test*

тетра́дь — *notebook (female)*

упражне́ние — *exercise*

учёбник — *textbook*

це́рковь — *church (female)*

часть — *part (female)*

шко́ла — *school*

язы́к — *language, tongue*

Verbs
Что де́лать?

говори́ть (говорю́, говори́шь, говоря́т) — *to speak*

де́лать (де́лаю, де́лаешь, де́лают) — *to do, make*

ду́мать (ду́маю, ду́маешь, ду́мают) — *to think*

знать (зна́ю, зна́ешь, зна́ют) — *to know*

игра́ть (игра́ю, игра́ешь, игра́ют) — *to play*

изуча́ть (изуча́ю, изуча́ешь, изуча́ют) — *to study a subject*

люби́ть (люблю́, лю́бишь, лю́бят) — *to love*

отдыха́ть (отдыха́ю, отдыха́ешь, отдыха́ют) — *to rest, relax*

повторя́ть (повторя́ю, повторя́ешь, повторя́ют) — *to repeat, review*

по́мнить (по́мню, по́мнишь, по́мнят) — *to remember*

понима́ть (понима́ю, понима́ешь, понима́ют) — *to understand*

рабо́тать (рабо́таю, рабо́таешь, рабо́тают) — *to work*

слу́шать (слу́шаю, слу́шаешь, слу́шают) — *to listen*

чита́ть (чита́ю, чита́ешь, чита́ют) — *to read*

Adjectives
Како́й?

англи́йский — *English*

ара́бский — *Arabic*

испа́нский — *Spanish*

италья́нский — *Italian*

кита́йский — *Chinese*

лито́вский — *Lithuanian*

неме́цкий — *German*

ру́сский — *Russian*

украи́нский — *Ukrainian*

францу́зский — *French*

япо́нский — *Japanese*

дома́шний — *home (adj.)*

просто́й — *simple*

тру́дный — *difficult, hard*

Adverbs with the opposite meaning
Как?

бы́стро — *fast, quickly*

ме́дленно — *slowly*

хорошо́ — *well*

пло́хо — *poorly, bad*

пра́вильно — *correct, right*

непра́вильно — *not right*

интере́сно — *interesting*

ску́чно — *it's boring*

ра́ньше — *before, earlier*

тепе́рь — *now*

Other adverbs
Как?

немно́го — *a little, not many*

непло́хо — *not bad; quite well*

норма́льно — *it's all right*

о́чень — *very*

свобо́дно — *freely, fluently*

Когда́?

вчера́ — *yesterday*

сего́дня — *today*

за́втра — *tomorrow*

Personal Pronouns
Кто?

я — *I*

ты — *you (singular, informal)*

мы — *we*

вы — *you (plural, formal)*

он — *he*

она́ — *she*

оно́ — *it*

они́ — *they*

его́ (него after a preposition) — *his*

её (неё after a preposition) — *her*

их (них after a preposition) — *their*

Prepositions

из — *from*

по — *by*

Conjunctions

а — *but, and*

и — *and*

и́ли — *or*

но — *but*

Phrases — Фра́зы

Рад познако́миться! — *Glad to meet you!*

Знако́мьтесь! — *Please meet!*

У кого́ (есть)...? Who has... ?

У меня́ (есть) — *I have*

У тебя́ (есть) — *You have*

У него́ (есть) *He has*

У неё (есть) *She has*

У нас (есть) *We have*

У вас (есть) *You (plural) have*

У них (есть) *They have*

Урок 1

его́ is pronounced **йиво́**

Её зову́т Ма́ша.
Она́ студе́нтка.
Она́ из Росси́и.

Её зову́т Юми.
Она́ певи́ца.
Она́ из Япо́нии.

Его́ зову́т То́мас.
Он музыка́нт.
Он из Кана́ды.

Отку́да вы? Where are you from?

Отку́да вы? — Я из Кана́ды.
Отку́да Ма́ша? — Она́ из Росси́и.

To say where you are from, change the name of the country as shown below.

Англи**я**	— из Англи**и**	**я** → **и**
Кана́д**а**	— из Кана́д**ы**	**а** → **ы**
Ме́ксик**а**	— из Ме́ксик**и**	**а** → **и** (after к, г, ш)

You will learn more about noun endings as you progress. For now, follow this model, and ask your teacher to help you with endings for names of places that don't have **а** or **я** at the end.

2.1–1. А. Отку́да ты? Ask 2-3 classmates where are they from.

Б. Ask your teacher where is he/she from. Remember to be polite/formal.

В. Отку́да он? Отку́да она́? Say where these people are from.

Образе́ц: Ка́рлос, Испа́ния. Ка́рлос **из** Испа́ни**и**.

1. Сюза́нна, Да́ния
2. Тиму́р, Ту́рция
3. Хосе́, Аргенти́на
4. Джейн, Аме́рика
5. Еле́на, Гре́ция
6. Джон, Австра́лия
7. Мо́ника, По́льша
8. Мо́рган, Кана́да
9. Ива́н, Росси́я
10. Ке́йко, Япо́ния

Профе́ссии. Talking about Professions and Occupations

Кто вы по профе́ссии? — Я журнали́ст.

Кто по профе́ссии Юми? — Она́ певи́ца.

по профе́ссии — *by profession*, you will learn this structure later on

Professions and occupations in Russian may have two forms: masculine and feminine.

он — она́

актёр — актри́са	*actor — actress*
пев́ец — певи́ца	*singer*
спортсме́н — спортсме́нка	*sportsman*
танцо́р — балери́на	*ballet dancer*
студе́нт — студе́нтка	*university or college student*
шко́льник — шко́льница	*elementary, middle and high school student*

Most professions, however, have only one masculine form used for both: males and females.

он, она́

музыка́нт	*musician*	президе́нт	*president*
врач	*doctor*	бизнесме́н	*businessman*
инжене́р	*engineer*	компози́тор	*composer*
профе́ссор	*professor*	космона́вт	*astronaut*

Some professions have optional feminine forms used mostly in colloquial Russian:

он — она́ *(optional)*

учи́тель — учи́тельница	*school teacher*
преподава́тель — преподава́тельница	*university or college teacher*
писа́тель — писа́тельница	*writer*
журнали́ст — журнали́стка	*journalist*

Поговори́м! Let's talk!

2.1–2. Working with a partner, take turns asking and answering questions about the people below.

1. Как его́ зову́т? Как её зову́т?
2. Отку́да он? Отку́да она́?
3. Кто он по профе́ссии? Кто она по профе́ссии?

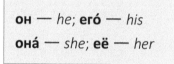

он — *he*; **его́** — *his*
она́ — *she*; **её** — *her*

Карл, Герма́ния

Мо́ника, Испа́ния

Са́ра, Аме́рика

Джоа́на, Австра́лия

Си́монас, Литва́

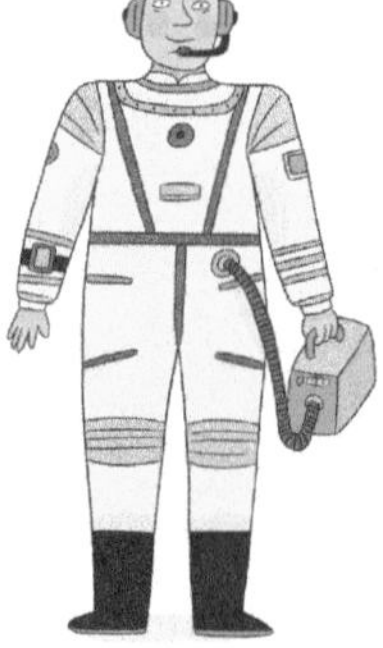

Па́трик, Фра́нция

Андре́й и Ири́на, Росси́я

Жизнь в Росси́и: лю́ди, исто́рия, культу́ра
Professions and Gender

Many professions and occupations are noticeably divided between genders in Russia. Women dominate in services and socio-cultural sphere of childcare, teaching, social science, and medicine. Men dominate within heavy industries that were traditionally male, such as coal, lumber, mineral extraction, machinery, and electric power industries.

Although women fully participate in working life, men predominantly occupy all levels of decision-making and top-level positions, even in the occupations that employed mostly women. For example, in Russian, a majority of nurses, physicians, technicians, and teachers are females; in contrast, the majority of head doctors, chief engineers, chief executives, and school principals are males.

Russian language reflects this gender-occupation distribution by means of feminine suffixes added to professions commonly occupied by women: **учи́тельница** — *teacher*, **продавщи́ца** — *shop assistant*, **журнали́стка** — *journalist*, which exist alongside with male forms: **учи́тель, продаве́ц, журнали́ст**. Such feminine forms remain colloquial and masculine nouns are used in formal and written language.

Professions where men still dominate do not receive a colloquial female form and one word — a masculine gender noun — is used for both men and women employees: **инжене́р** — *engineer*, **юри́ст** — *lawyer*, **космона́вт** — *astronaut*, **мини́стр** — *minister*, **президе́нт** — *president*. The majority of words for professions in Russian language are masculine gender nouns.

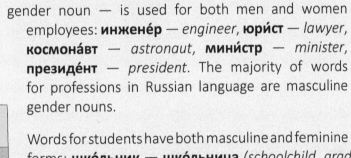

Words for students have both masculine and feminine forms: **шко́льник — шко́льница** *(schoolchild, grade school student)*, **студе́нт — студе́нтка** *(university/college student)*, **аспира́нт — аспира́нтка** *(graduate student)*.

Occupations where males and females traditionally play equal roles have two forms in formal and colloquial Russian: **актёр** — *actor* and **актри́са** — *actress*, **певе́ц** — *male singer* and **певи́ца** — *female singer.* This is also true for various sports occupations: **спортсме́н — спортсме́нка** *(athlete)*, **тенниси́ст — тенниси́стка** *(tennis player)*, **фигури́ст — фигури́стка** *(figure skater)*, **гимна́ст — гимна́стка** *(gymnast)*, etc.

Урок 2

Grammatical Gender of Nouns

Regular Forms

You already know that Russian nouns belong to one of three genders: masculine, feminine, or neuter. The gender is easy to tell by looking at the noun's ending in the nominative case (the basic form in which the word is introduced in a dictionary).

A noun is **masculine** if it ends **in a consonant** (the ending is often marked as **Ø** in textbooks).
A noun is **feminine** if it ends in **-а**, **-я**.
A noun is **neuter** if it ends in **-о**, **-е**.

	Masculine	Feminine	Neuter
Hard Stem	журна́л — *journal*	кни́г**а** — *book*	сло́в**о** — *word*
Soft Stem	музе́**й** — *museum*	ста́ть**я** — *article*	пла́ть**е** — *dress*
	-Ø/-й	-а/-я	-о/-е

2.2–1. Identify the grammatical gender of the following nouns. Can you tell what each word means?

пла́тье	апельси́н	нож
уро́к	семья́	ло́жка
профе́ссия	я́блоко	ча́шка
ру́чка	чай	сыр
окно́	кафе́	мёд
оши́бка	у́тро	хлеб
каранда́ш	ве́чер	ма́сло

- **Gender of nouns in -ь**

  Nouns ending in -ь can be masculine or feminine. Later, you will learn some tips to help you predict their gender (For example, all months are masculine and thus, **ию́нь**, **ию́ль**, **янва́рь**, etc. are masculine nouns). For now, memorize the gender of such nouns when you learn the word. The word list below introduces the gender of some common nouns in -ь you have learned in previous chapter.

Masculine	**Feminine**
календа́р**ь** — *calendar*	тетра́д**ь** — *notebook*
слова́р**ь** — *dictionary*	доч**ь** — *daughter*
ден**ь** — *day*	ноч**ь** — *night*
дожд**ь** — rain	жизн**ь** — *life*
	любо́в**ь** — *love*
	це́рков**ь** — *church*
	част**ь** — *part*

  All nouns in **-ь** have their gender marked as (*m.*) or (*f.*) in dictionaries and vocabulary lists.

- **Masculine nouns in -a**

  Masculine nouns ending in-a/-я are exceptions. Most common ones include:

  - male family members: **па́па** — *dad*, **дя́дя** — *uncle*, **де́душка** — *grandpa*;
  - male nicknames such as **Ва́ня** (from Ива́н), **Ди́ма** (from Дми́трий), **Серёжа** (from Серге́й) and others.

  These nouns always refer to a male person and take masculine modifiers (**мой па́па**). The pronoun **он** is used to substitute for such noun: Где **Ва́ня**? — Вот **он**.

- **Professions and Gender**

  Some professions have masculine and feminine forms to match with person's gender (**актёр — актри́са, студе́нт — студе́нтка**). Many professions, however, have only one (usually masculine) form: **врач, инжене́р, юри́ст**. These words take a masculine modifier regardless the physical gender of the person but the pronouns **он** and **она́** reflect the person's gender:

  Это Ива́н Петро́вич. **Он мой** врач.

  Это Анна Алекса́ндровна. **Она́ мой** врач.

2.2–2. Which pronoun (**он**, **она́** или **оно́**) would you choose to substitute for the following nouns? Pay attention to the exceptions, and look up the gender of nouns ending in **-ь**.

дом	сло́во	муж	семья́	студе́нтка
день	любо́вь	жена́	сын	учи́тель
ночь	жизнь	па́па	дочь	певи́ца
пла́тье	Ди́ма	дя́дя	де́душка	певе́ц
дождь	Ма́ша	тётя	ба́бушка	президе́нт

Поговори́м! Let's talk!

2.2–3. Working with a partner, ask where these things and people are and point to them saying: Вот он. Вот она́. Вот оно́. Take turns asking and answering.

Кни́га, слова́рь, пла́тье, рюкза́к, де́душка, тетра́дь, семья́, врач, музе́й, календа́рь, це́рковь, па́па, дочь, сын, муж, жена́.

Образе́ц: Где кни́га? — Вот она́.

2.2–4. Study the vocabulary below that you will often use in your Russian classroom, and identify the grammatical gender (**он**, **она́**, **оно́**) of each word.

Сло́во	Перево́д	Род (Gender)
кни́га	*book*	___________
газе́та	*newspaper*	___________
журна́л	*journal*	___________
слова́рь	*dictionary*	___________
учё́бник	*textbook*	___________
тетра́дь	*workbook*	___________
страни́ца	*page*	___________
пра́вило	*rule*	___________
упражне́ние	*exercise*	___________
предложе́ние	*sentence*	___________
уро́к	*lesson*	___________
диало́г	*dialogue*	___________
дома́шняя рабо́та	*homework*	___________
письмо́	*letter*	___________
статья́	*article*	___________
расска́з	*story*	___________
ска́зка	*fairytale*	___________
рома́н	*novel*	___________
исто́рия	*story, history*	___________
перево́д	*translation*	___________
сло́во	*word*	___________
образе́ц	*model*	___________
текст	*text*	___________
вопро́с	*question*	___________
отве́т	*answer*	___________
тест	*test*	___________

Урок 3

Russian Verbs. The Present Tense. Introduction

Я люблю́ **чита́ть**.

Я **чита́ю** журна́л.

The Infinitive

The infinitive is the basic form of the verb. In all dictionaries, verbs are listed in the infinitive form.
In English, the infinitive is composed of two words: ***to read***. In a sentence, the infinitive is never used without another verb: *I like* ***to read***. *It is fun* ***to swim***.

In Russian, the infinitive is a single word. Most infinitives end in **-ть**: **чита́ть** — *to read*, **знать** — *to know*, **изуча́ть** — *to study*. Like in English, Russian infinitive is used in a sentence with another verb:

Я люблю́ **чита́ть**. *I like* ***to read***.

The Present Tense

Russian present tense corresponds to different present tense aspects in English: present simple (*I read*), present progressive (*I am reading*), present perfect progressive (*I have been reading*). Compare:

In Russian	In English
Я чита́ю	*I read.* *I am reading.* *I have been reading.*

Verb Conjugation in English

A conjugation is the term used for a list of six possible forms of the verb, one for each of the subject pronouns — *I, we, you* (sing.), *you* (pl.), *he/she, they*. English verbs change very little as they conjugate:

Singular		Plural	
1st person	I read.	1st person	We read.
2nd person	You read.	2nd person	You read.
3rd person	He/She reads.	3rd person	They read.

As you see, the only form that differs from others is the 3rd person singular: *he/she reads*.

Verb Conjugation in Russian

Russian verbs in the present tense have six **different** forms (one unique form for each of the subject pronouns: я, ты, он/она/кто, мы, вы, они). In addition, Russian has two patterns of verb conjugation:

- **1st conjugation** (also known as **-е** conjugation)
- **2nd conjugation** (also known as **-и** conjugation)

The following chart provides the list of personal pronouns and shows the present tense endings of the 1st conjugation verb **чита́ть** — *to read* and the 2nd conjugation verb **говори́ть** — *to speak*.

Personal Pronoun	1st conjugation чита́-**ть**	2nd conjugation говор-**и́ть**
я	чита́-**ю**	говор-**ю́**
ты	чита́-**ешь**	говор-**и́шь**
он, она́, кто	чита́-**ет**	говор-**и́т**
мы	чита́-**ем**	говор-**и́м**
вы	чита́-**ете**	говор-**и́те**
они́	чита́-**ют**	говор-**я́т**

Most Russian verbs belong to the 1st conjugation; the 2nd conjugation pattern is less common. All verbs introduced in this chapter (except **говори́ть** — *to speak* and **по́мнить** — *to remember*) are 1st conjugation verbs. As you learn a new verb, you must pay attention to its conjugation pattern: 1st or 2nd.

2.3–1. Кто что чита́ет? Who reads what? Complete the sentences with the correct forms of **чита́ть** — *to read* and translate them into English. Refer to exercise 2.2–4 for vocabulary review.

Образе́ц: Я ________________ письмо́. Я **чита́ю** письмо́.

1. Мы ________________ текст.
2. Они́ ________________ диало́г.
3. Что вы ________________?
4. Что ты ________________?
5. Я ________________ предложе́ние.

6. Он ______________ упражне́ние.
7. Кто ______________ уче́бник?
8. Ба́бушка ______________ журна́л.
9. Студе́нт ______________ пра́вило.
10. Ма́ша и Ди́ма ______________ расска́з.

To form the present tense,

1st conjugation: remove two final letters (**-ть**) from the infinitive and add appropriate ending as shown in **чита́ть** chart.

2nd conjugation: remove three final letters (**-ить**) from the infinitive and add appropriate ending as shown in **говори́ть** chart.

More 1st conjugation verbs

знать	*to know*
ду́мать	*to think*
понима́ть	*to understand*
изуча́ть	*to study*
рабо́тать	*to work*
де́лать	*to do*
отдыха́ть	*to rest*
слу́шать	*to listen*
расска́зывать	*to tell (a story)*
игра́ть	*to play*

More 2nd conjugation verbs

по́мнить	*to remember*

2.3–2. Как по-ру́сски? How would you say it in Russian? Use **чита́ть** as a model. Refer to the verb list above for translation of new verbs.

Образе́ц: I read. — **Я чита́ю.**

1. I know / You (sing.) know / He knows
2. I think / You (sing.) think / She thinks
3. We understand / You (pl.) understand / They understand
4. We study / You (pl.) study / They study
5. I work / You (sing.) work / He works
6. We do / You (pl.) do / They do
7. I rest / You (sing.) rest / She rests
8. We listen / You (pl.) listen / They listen
9. He tells / They tell / You (pl.) tell
10. I play / She plays / They play

2.3–3. Как по-ру́сски? How would you say it in Russian? Use **говори́ть** as a model.

1. I remember / You (sing.) remember / He remembers
2. We remember / You (pl.) remember / They (pl.) remember

2.3–4. Complete the sentences with the correct form of the verb in parenthesis.

Образе́ц: Он ______________ (слу́шать) ра́дио. Он **слу́шает** ра́дио.

1. Я ______________ (знать) э́то сло́во.
2. Вы ______________ (понима́ть) э́то пра́вило?
3. Мы ______________ (изуча́ть) ру́сский язы́к.
4. Они́ ______________ (слу́шать) диало́г.
5. Кто ______________ (чита́ть) обра́зец?
6. Па́па за́втра ______________ (рабо́тать) и́ли ______________ (отдыха́ть)?
7. Что вы ______________ (де́лать) ве́чером?
8. Ты ______________ (слу́шать) ра́дио? — Нет, я ______________(ду́мать).
9. Ма́ша ______________ (расска́зывать) о себе́.
10. Я ______________ (по́мнить) э́то сло́во.
11. А ты ______________ (по́мнить)?
12. Я ______________ (говори́ть) «Приве́т».
13. А что ты ______________ (говори́ть)?

> **о себе** translates as:
> *about myself*
> *about yourself*
> *about himself/herself*
> *about ourselves*
> *about yourselves*
> *about themselves*

Negating the action in Russian

Negating in Russian is simple. Russian does not use auxiliary verbs (like English '*to do*' or '*to be*') to form a negative statement. Therefore, ***I don't read*** translates as **Я не чита́ю**; ***I'm not listening:*** **Я не слу́шаю.**

> To negate an action, simply add **не** before the verb:
>
> Я **не** рабо́таю. *I **don't** work.*
> Я **не** понима́ю. *I **don't** understand.*

2.3–5. Negate the following actions.

1. Я зна́ю э́то пра́вило.
2. Он понима́ет текст.
3. Она́ изуча́ет англи́йский язы́к.
4. Они́ слу́шают диало́г.

2.3–6. Что вы де́лаете и что не де́лаете? What are you doing and what are you not doing? Say what you are doing and what you are not doing right now. Make at least five short statements about yourself. Use the verbs and nouns you are learning in this chapter.

Я ____

____

____

Поговори́м! Let's talk!

2.3–7. These people are doing different things. Working with a partner, take turns asking and answering the questions as in the model.

Образе́ц:

— Мари́я слу́шает ра́дио?

— Нет, она́ не слу́шает ра́дио, она́ чита́ет журна́л.

— Ка́тя рабо́тает?

— ________________.

— Андре́й отдыха́ет?

— ____________________.

— Ди́ма и Ва́ня слу́шают текст?

— ________________.

For the following two images, create your own questions and answers. Have fun joking and improvising, but stick to the verbs and sentence structures you know.

— ____________________?

— ____________________.

— ____________________?

— ____________________.

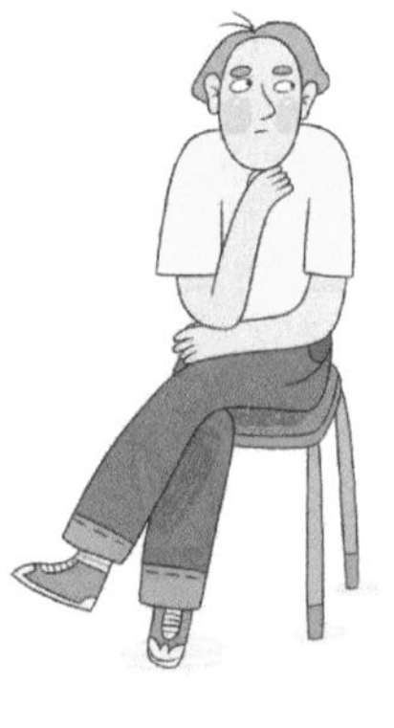

Чита́йте те́кст. Ру́сская семья́.

Это ру́сская семья́*. Вот Иван Петро́вич, а э́то его́	**family*
жена́* — Анна Алекса́ндровна. Ива́н Петро́вич —	**wife*
инжене́р. Анна Алекса́ндровна — врач.	
А э́то их* де́ти*: дочь Ма́ша и сын Ди́ма. Ма́ша — студе́нтка, а Ди́ма — шко́льник.	**their; *children*
Сего́дня у них* го́сти*: То́мас из Кана́ды и Юми из Япо́нии.	**they have; *guests*
То́мас и Юми изуча́ют* ру́сский язы́к*.	**study; *Russian language*
Они́ хорошо́ чита́ют*, но пло́хо* понима́ют* по-ру́сски.	**read; *poorly; *understand*

сего́дня — *today* is pronounced с**и**во́дня

Вопро́сы

1. Кто э́то?
2. Кто врач, а кто инжене́р?
3. Как зову́т дочь? Кто она́?
4. Ди́ма студе́нт и́ли шко́льник?
5. Кто у них сего́дня?
6. Отку́да То́мас и отку́да Юми?
7. Что изуча́ют То́мас и Юми?

Слу́шайте и чита́йте диало́ги.

1. Знако́мьтесь — э́то мои́ друзья́!

Ма́ша:	Ма́ма, па́па, приве́т! Знако́мьтесь — э́то мои́ друзья́: То́мас и Юми.
Анна Алекса́ндровна:	До́брый ве́чер. Меня́ зову́т Анна Алекса́ндровна.
То́мас:	Здра́вствуйте. Очень прия́тно!
Ива́н Петро́вич:	Ива́н Петро́вич. Рад познако́миться.
Ма́ша:	А где Ди́ма?
Анна Алекса́ндровна:	Вот он.

2. Отку́да вы? Кто вы по профе́ссии?

Ива́н Петро́вич:	То́мас, отку́да вы?	
То́мас:	Я из Кана́ды.	
Ива́н Петро́вич:	А кто вы по профе́ссии?	
То́мас:	Я музыка́нт. А ещё* я студе́нт. А вы?	*also
Ива́н Петро́вич:	Я инжене́р.	
То́мас:	Интересно*.	*it is interesting

3. Вы давно́ изуча́ете ру́сский язы́к? *How long have you been learning Russian for?*

Анна Алекса́ндровна:	Юми, кто вы по профе́ссии?	
Юми:	Я певи́ца и студе́нтка. А вы?	
Анна Алекса́ндровна:	Я врач, а мой муж* Ива́н Петро́вич — инжене́р.	*husband
Юми:	Очень интере́сно!	
Анна Алекса́ндровна:	А вы давно́* изуча́ете ру́сский язы́к?	*long (time)
Юми:	Нет, не о́чень. Я изуча́ю ру́сский то́лько оди́н год*. Я хорошо́ чита́ю, но пло́хо понима́ю.	*only one year

Вопро́сы к диало́гам. Answer the questions based on what you learned in the dialogues above.

1. Кто по профе́ссии То́мас?
2. Кто по профе́ссии Юми?
3. Кто по профе́ссии Анна Алекса́ндровна и кто Ива́н Петро́вич?
4. Юми давно́ изуча́ет ру́сский язы́к?
5. Юми хорошо́ понима́ет по-ру́сски?

2.3–8. Расскажи́те о себе́. Tell about yourself. Как вас зову́т? Отку́да вы? Кто вы по профе́ссии? Pick two or three of your family members (ма́ма, па́па, ба́бушка, де́душка, брат, сестра́, дя́дя, тётя) and tell what their professions are.

2.3–9. Pretend you are someone else. Pick a country of origin and a profession. Use vocabulary introduced in this chapter to tell your classmates about your "pretend self".

Поговори́м! Let's talk!

2.3–10. Working with a partner, create a dialogue. Use vocabulary and phrases introduced in this and previous chapters. Be sure to include the following elements:

- greet each other in a formal way,
- introduce yourselves,
- find out where your partner is from and what his/her profession is (You can use a pretend name and profession.),
- arrange for a meeting tomorrow at home at a certain time in the evening (refer to exercise 1.5-14. in Урок 5, Тема 1), and
- finish the conversation politely.

Memorize and act out your dialogue for the rest of the class.

Урок 4

Question Как? How? Adverbs

Ма́ша **хорошо́** чита́ет.

— **Как** То́мас чита́ет?
— То́мас чита́ет **хорошо́**.

Adverbs

To say **how** someone reads, listens, understands, etc., an adverb should be used:

Ма́ша **хорошо́** чита́ет. *Masha reads **well**.*

Most Russian adverbs end in **-o**. Study the list of common adverbs below. Read them aloud.

бы́стро	*fast, quickly*	ме́дленно	*slowly*
интере́сно	*interesting(ly)*	ску́чно	*boring*
пра́вильно	*correct(ly), properly*	непра́вильно	*incorrect(ly), wrong*
хорошо́	*well*	пло́хо	*poorly, not well*
непло́хо	*not bad*	немно́го	*a little*
свобо́дно	*fluently*		

Word order

Put adverbs like **хорошо́** before verbs when you are making a statement on how one reads, works, etc.:

Я **ме́дленно** чита́ю. *I read slowly.*

То́мас **хорошо́** чита́ет, но **пло́хо** понима́ет по-ру́сски. *Thomas reads well but understands Russian poorly.*

However, in answering the question **Как** — *How*, put such adverbs after verbs:

— **Как** ты чита́ешь по-ру́сски? — ***How** do you read in Russian?*
— Я чита́ю **ме́дленно**. — *I read **slowly**.*

2.4–1. Как? Complete the sentences using adverbs with the opposite meaning.

Образе́ц:

— Как они́ чита́ют?
— Студе́нт чита́ет ме́дленно, а преподава́тель чита́ет **бы́стро**.

1. — Как они́ понима́ют вопро́с?
   — Ма́ша понима́ет вопро́с хорошо́, а То́мас ____________________.
2. — Как они́ рабо́тают?
   — Па́па рабо́тает бы́стро, а сын ____________________.
3. — Как они́ расска́зывают?
   — Андре́й расска́зывает ску́чно, а Серге́й ____________________.
4. — Как они́ понима́ют э́то предложе́ние?
   — То́мас понима́ет предложе́ние пра́вильно, а Джон ____________.

2.4–2. Complete the sentences with the correct form of the verb **говори́ть**. Refer to Урок 3 to review 2nd conjugation forms. Translate these sentences into English.

по-англи́йски — *in English*
по-ру́сски — *in Russian*

1. Я свобо́дно ____________________ по-англи́йски.
2. Ты хорошо́ ____________________ по-ру́сски?
3. Вы ____________________ по-англи́йски?
4. Мой па́па свобо́дно ____________________ по-ру́сски.
5. Де́душка и ба́бушка немно́го ____________________ по-англи́йски.
6. Мы ме́дленно ____________________ по-ру́сски, а преподава́тель ____________________ о́чень бы́стро.

о́чень — *very*

2.4–3. О себе́. About yourself. Comment on some of your Russian language skills. Use the following adverbs: хорошо́, пло́хо, бы́стро, ме́дленно, пра́вильно, непра́вильно, свобо́дно, немно́го.

1. Я ____________________ чита́ю по-ру́сски.
2. Я ____________________ де́лаю упражне́ние.
3. Я ____________________ понима́ю вопро́с.
4. Я ____________________ расска́зываю текст.
5. Я ____________________ говорю́ по-ру́сски.

Разговóр

2.4–4. Listen to the dialogue and fill in the missing words.

Мáша: Дóбрый день! Меня́ зовýт Мáша. А вас?

Тóмас: А меня́ Тóмас.

Мáша: ____________________ Тóмас? Из Англии?

Тóмас: Нет, я ____________________.

Мáша: Как интерéсно! А вы давнó изучáете рýсский язы́к?

Тóмас: Извини́те, я ____________________. Говори́те, пожáлуйста, ____________________.

Мáша: Хорошó. Тóмас, вы давнó изучáете рýсский язы́к?

Тóмас: Нет, не óчень. Я изучáю рýсский тóлько оди́н год. Я ____________________ читáю, но ____________________ понимáю и мéдленно говорю́. А вы ____________________ по-англи́йски?

Мáша: Да, немнóго ____________________. Я изучáю англи́йский четы́ре гóда.

Урок 5

Я говорю́ по-ру́сски. Discussing Language Skills

— Вы говори́те **по-ру́сски**?

— Да, я говорю́ **по-ру́сски**.

The words like **по-ру́сски** and **по-англи́йски** are adverbs. They are used to talk about language skills: **говори́ть** — *to speak*, **чита́ть** — *to read*, **понима́ть** — *to understand*, **писа́ть** — *to write*.

Such adverbs are formed from adjectives **ру́сский**, **англи́йский**, etc. Here is the list of some common languages:

Adjective **...-ский**	Adverb **по- ... -ски**	Language
англи́й**ский**	по-англи́йски	English
ара́б**ский**	по-ара́бски	Arabic
испа́н**ский**	по-испа́нски	Spanish
италья́н**ский**	по-италья́нски	Italian
кита́й**ский**	по-кита́йски	Chinese
лито́в**ский**	по-лито́вски	Lithuanian
неме́ц**кий**	по-неме́цки	German
ру́с**ский**	по-ру́сски	Russian
украи́н**ский**	по-украи́нски	Ukrainian
францу́з**ский**	по-францу́зски	French
япо́н**ский**	по-япо́нски	Japanese

Many more adjectives and adverbs are formed this way from proper nouns. Compare:

Аме́рика *America* → америка́**нский** *American* → **по-**америка́**нски** *in the American way*

Кана́да *Canada* → кана́д**ский** *Canadian* → **по-**кана́д**ски** *in the Canadian way*

Москва́ *Moscow* → моско́в**ский** *Moscovian* → **по-**моско́в**ски** *in the Moscovian way*

Ки́ев *Kiev* → ки́ев**ский** *Kievan* → **по-**ки́ев**ски** *in the Kievan way*

> Only proper nouns are capitalized in Russian; adjectives and adverbs derived from proper nouns are not capitalized.

Adjectives and adverbs that do not refer to a language are used for "ways of doing things". For example, in restaurant menus, you might see an expression like "ко́фе по-америка́нски".

Very common such adverbs are used in restaurant menus:

ко́фе по-америка́нски — *coffee prepared the American way*

карто́фель по-кана́дски — *potatoes prepared the Canadian way*

ры́ба по-моско́вски — *fish prepared the Moscow way*

котле́ты по-ки́евски — *cutlets prepared the Kiev way*

2.5–1. What languages do these people speak? Complete the sentences as in the model. You can use one or more languages with or without an adverb.

Образе́ц: Мой брат ... Мой брат <u>гово́рит по-англи́йски и немно́го по-францу́зски</u>.

1. Моя́ ма́ма ...
2. Мой па́па ...
3. Ке́йко и Юми из Япо́нии ...
4. Музыка́нт из Кана́ды ...
5. Пев́ец из Ме́ксики ...
6. Компози́тор из Ита́лии ...
7. Бизнесме́н из Аме́рики ...
8. Балери́на из Росси́и ...
9. Писа́тель из Герма́нии ...
10. Я ...

2.5–2. Вы говори́те or Ты говори́шь? How would you ask these people if they speak English?

1. your Russian friend's grandma
2. your Russian friend's little brother
3. a waitress in a restaurant
4. your new Russian teacher
5. a Russian doctor
6. a classmate of your age
7. a group of foreign students
8. a group of Russian children

Ты-forms are used to address one person informally (friends, close relatives, children). **Вы-forms** are used to address someone you don't know very well or two and more people.

Remember to change verbs to agree with the pronoun:

- Вы говор**и́те**...? Вы чита́**ете**...?
- Ты говор**и́шь**...? Ты чита́**ешь**...?

2.5–3. Judging by the countries these people live in, tell what languages they speak.

Образе́ц: Си́монас из Литвы́. Я ду́маю, что он говори́т по-лито́вски.

1. Мо́ника, Испа́ния
2. Юми, Япо́ния
3. Са́ра, Аме́рика
4. Карл, Герма́ния
5. Джоа́на, Австра́лия
6. Си́монас, Литва́
7. Па́трик, Фра́нция
8. Андре́й и Ири́на, Росси́я

Я ду́маю, что ...
I think that...

The verb писа́ть — to write

Some verbs have their present tense stems different from the infinitives. The verb **писа́ть** is one of them. Memorize the present tense forms of this verb:

Personal Pronoun	1st conjugation писа́**ть**
я	пиш-у́
ты	пи́ш-**ешь**
он, она́, кто	пи́ш-**ет**
мы	пи́ш-**ем**
вы	пи́ш-**ете**
они́	пи́ш-**ут**

Notes

- -у in the я and они forms: я пишу́, они пи́шут;
- final syllable stress for the infinitive and я form that moves to the preceding syllable for the other forms.

2.5–4. Complete the sentences with the correct form of the verb **писа́ть**. Translate these sentences into English.

1. Я бы́стро ______________________ по-англи́йски.
2. Ты ______________________ по-францу́зски?
3. Мы ме́дленно ______________________ по-ру́сски.
4. Вы ______________________ по-япо́нски?
5. Ма́ша непло́хо ______________________ по-англи́йски.
6. Юми и То́мас хорошо́ ______________________ по-ру́сски.

2.5–5. О себé. About yourself. How do they write in these languages? Combine the elements below to make meaningful sentences. Use the correct form of **писáть**. Do not change the word order.

Я	хорошó	писáть	по-англи́йски
Мой друг	плóхо		по-францу́зски
Моя́ подру́га	бы́стро		по-ру́сски
Мой брат	мéдленно		по-испáнски
Моя́ сестрá	не		по-немéцки
Преподавáтель			
Моя́ кóшка			

Урок 6

Russian Verbs. Past Tense

Что вы де́лали?

Мы говори́ли и чита́ли по-ру́сски.

The past tense is used to talk about actions that occurred at some time in the past. Russian past tense corresponds to different past tense aspects in English:

In Russian	In English
Я рабо́тал.	*I worked.* *I have worked.* *I was working.* *I had been working.* *I used to work.*

Russian past tense verbs do not conjugate but they reflect the gender (masculine, feminine, or neuter) and number (plural) of the subject. To form the past tense, remove the infinitive ending **-ть** and replace it with past tense endings like it is shown in the following chart.

Gender, number		1st conjugation чита́**ть**	2nd conjugation говор**и́ть**
m.	он (кто, я, ты)	чита́-**л**	говори́-**л**
f.	она́ (я, ты)	чита́-**ла**	говори́-**ла**
n.	оно́	чита́-**ло**	говори́-**ло**
pl.	они́ (мы, вы)	чита́-**ли**	говори́-**ли**

я чита́л

я чита́ла

In the past tense:

- There is no conjugation.
- Verbs agree with their subjects in gender and number.
- The past tense is formed from the infinitive (regardless verb's conjugation type) and not from the present tense (**чита́ть — он чита́л**, **говори́ть — он говори́л**). This is most noticeable in verbs with irregular present tense stem like **писа́ть**. Compare: **он пи́шет** (present) and **он писа́л** (past).
- **Кто** requires the masculine past tense form:

  Кто чита́л рома́н «Анна Каре́нина»?
- **Я** and **ты** can go with either masculine of feminine form depending on the physical gender of the person:

  Ты чита́л? Ты чита́ла?

  Я чита́л. Я чита́ла.
- **Вы** always requires the plural past tense form (Grammatically for **вы**, there is no difference between addressing many people or one person in a formal polite way.):

  Ива́н Петро́вич, **вы чита́ли** рома́н «Анна Каре́нина?»

  То́мас, Юми, **вы чита́ли** рома́н «Анна Каре́нина»?

In addition to tense, Russian has **Aspect**. The concept of aspect can be roughly defined as an attitude toward action in time. Russian verbs have two aspects: imperfective (action in process) and perfective (completed action). The concept of aspect will be introduced to you later. For the time being, all verbs in your active vocabulary are **imperfective verbs**.

2.6–1. Complete the sentences with the past tense forms of verbs in parenthesis.

1. Что вы ____________________ (де́лать) вчера́ ве́чером?
2. Ма́ма ____________________ (чита́ть) журна́л.
3. Па́па ____________________ (рабо́тать).
4. Де́душка и ба́бушка ____________________ (слу́шать) конце́рт.
5. Брат ____________________ (игра́ть).
6. Сестра́ ____________________ (писа́ть) упражне́ние.
7. Я ____________________ (отдыха́ть).

The verb *to be* in the past tense

Ве́чером ма́ма была́ до́ма. *In the evening mum was at home.*

As you already know, the verb *to be* is absent in present tense. In the past tense, **быть** — *to be* is formed and functions like any other verb:

	бы**ть** — *to be*
он, кто	бы-**л**
она́	бы-**ла́**
оно́	бы́-**ло**
они́	бы́-**ли**

Note the end stress in the feminine form: **была́**.

2.6–2. Кто вчера́ был до́ма? Когда́? Во ско́лько? Say who was at home yesterday. When? At what time? Use the past tense of the verb *to be* to complete sentences.

1. Утром в де́вять часо́в ма́ма ________ до́ма.
2. Днём в три часа́ брат ________ до́ма.
3. Днём в три часа́ тётя Та́ня то́же* ________ до́ма. *also
4. Ве́чером в пять часо́в дя́дя Пе́тя ________ до́ма.
5. Ве́чером в шесть часо́в па́па ________ до́ма.
6. Ве́чером в семь часо́в ба́бушка и де́душка ________ до́ма.
7. Но́чью вся* семья́ ________ до́ма. *the whole
8. — Когда́ вы ________ до́ма?
9. — ____________________ я ________ дома.

2.6–3. Complete the story using the past tense forms of verbs in parenthesis.

Вчера́ ве́чером Ива́н Петро́вич, Анна Алекса́ндровна, Ма́ша и Ди́ма ________________ (быть) до́ма. Что они́ ____________________ (де́лать)?

Ива́н Петро́вич ____________________ (отдыха́ть). Анна Алекса́ндровна ________________________ (слу́шать) конце́рт по телевизо́ру*. *on TV

Ма́ша ____________________ (чита́ть) рома́н по-англи́йски. Ди́ма ________________ (де́лать) уро́ки* и ________________ (игра́ть). *do homework

2.6–4. Ра́ньше..., а тепе́рь... *Before... but now...* Tell how the students' language skills have improved. Use verbs in parenthesis in the past tense after **ра́ньше** and in the present tense after **а тепе́рь**.

Ра́ньше..., а тепе́рь... — *Before... but now*

1. Ра́ньше мы не ________________ (говори́ть) по-ру́сски, а тепе́рь немно́го* ________________ (говори́ть). *a little bit
2. Ра́ньше Та́ня пло́хо ________________ (понима́ть) по-англи́йски, а тепе́рь она́ о́чень хорошо́ ________________ (понима́ть).
3. Ра́ньше Юми пло́хо ________________ (чита́ть) по-ру́сски, а тепе́рь она́ о́чень хорошо́ ________________ (чита́ть).
4. Ра́ньше Са́ра не ________________ (понима́ть) по-япо́нски, а тепе́рь она́ непло́хо ________________ (понима́ть).
5. Ра́ньше я ________________, а тепе́рь ________________.

Разгово́р

2.6–5. Listen to the dialogue and fill in the missing words.

то́лько — *only*
то́же — *also*
всегда́ — *always*
в (**во**) — *in*

То́мас: Юми, ты давно́ ________________ ру́сский язы́к?

Юми: Нет, то́лько оди́н год. А ты?

То́мас: Я то́же ________________ ру́сский то́лько год.

Юми: Ты о́чень хорошо́ ________________. Я всегда́ тебя́ понима́ю.

То́мас: Спаси́бо. Я то́же хорошо́ понима́ю, когда́ ты говори́шь, но я ________________ понима́ю, когда́ говоря́т ру́сские.

Юми: А каки́е ещё языки́ ты ________________?

То́мас: Я изуча́л францу́зский язы́к. Я непло́хо говорю́, но пло́хо чита́ю ________________. А каки́е языки́ ты зна́ешь?

Юми: Я изуча́ла ________________ два го́да.

То́мас: Ты ________________ в Англии?

Юми: Да, была́. А ты ________________ во Фра́нции?

То́мас: Нет, я ________________ во Фра́нции. Я изуча́л францу́зский в Кана́де.

Урок 7

Повторяем. Chapter 2 Review

This section summarizes what you should be able to understand and say after completing this chapter. For additional practice, vocabulary building and self-tests, please go to Спутник website.

1. Слушаем и понимаем

Each unit will introduce listening practice (monologues and conversations) where you can hear different people discussing the unit's topic. Do not try to understand everything! In these talks and conversations, there will be words and structures you don't know yet. Your goal is to get certain information and answer questions.

Listening tips:

- Before you listen, read and try to understand the questions first.
- Listen to the whole conversation and figure out what is being discussed.
- With questions in mind, listen again for specific information.
- Write down your answers. (You don't have to answer in full sentences.)
- Listen one more time to check your answers.

А. Маша рассказывает о себе. Listen to Masha's story, and answer the questions about her.

1. Откуда Маша?
2. Какой* язык она изучает? **what (kind)*
3. Что она любит* делать? **like, love*
4. Кто по профессии её папа и мама?
5. У неё есть брат или сестра?

Б. Юми рассказывает о себе. Listen to Yumi's story, and answer the questions about her.

1. What does the verb "петь" mean if певец/певица is a singer?
2. Откуда Юми?
3. Как Юми говорит по-английски?

4. Что она́ лю́бит де́лать?
5. Кто по профе́ссии ма́ма и па́па Юми?
6. Её сестра́ студе́нтка и́ли шко́льница?

В. То́мас расска́зывает о себе́. Listen to Thomas's story, and answer the questions about him.

1. What does "музыка́льная семья́" mean?
2. Отку́да То́мас?
3. Как он говори́т по-англи́йски и по-францу́зски?
4. То́мас давно́ изуча́ет ру́сский язы́к?
5. Кто по профе́ссии его́ ма́ма и па́па?
6. Check all musical instruments that Tomas plays:

а) пиани́но	г) саксофо́н
б) гита́ра	д) фле́йта
в) кларне́т	е) тромбо́н

Г. Разгово́р по-ру́сски. Listen to the conversation, and answer the questions. You don't have to understand everything!

Answer in Russian.

1. Кто хорошо́ говори́т по-англи́йски?
   а) студе́нты из Япо́нии
   б) Ма́ша
   в) Андре́й
2. Во ско́лько Ма́ше и Андре́ю ну́жно встре́титься?
   а) в де́вять часо́в
   б) в де́сять часо́в
   в) в двена́дцать часо́в

Answer in English.

3. What languages are being discussed?

4. What countries are mentioned?
5. What language doesn't Masha speak?
6. What kind of job does Andrei offer to Masha?
7. Does she agree to help?

Guessing and estimating

In **перево́дчик** the letter **д** is silent.

8. Can you guess what "**экску́рсия по Москве́**" mean?
9. What profession does the word **перево́дчик** refer to if **перево́д** means "*translation*"?

2. Чита́ем вслух

In this section, you will find long words broken into syllables. Read them aloud to master pronunciation. Phrases and intonation contours patterns follow the syllable reading exercise. The exercises are complemented by recordings posted on the book's website.

Слушаем и читаем

А. Practice reading the following words aloud. Listen to the recording, and try to self-correct your pronunciation.

го-во-ри́-т, слу́-ша-е-т, и-зу-ча́-е-т, расс-ка́-зы-ва-ет, по-ни-ма́-ет
го-во-ри́-ли, слу́-ша-ли, и-зу-ча́-ли, расс-ка́-зы-ва-ли, по-ни-ма́-ли

пе-ви́-ца, ин-же-не́р, шко́ль-ник, у-чи́-тель, у-чи́-тель-ни-ца, пре-по-да-ва́-тель, пре-по-да-ва́-тель-ни-ца, пи-са́-тель, пе-ре-во́-дчик, ком-по-зи́-тор

по-ру́-сски, по-ан-гли́й-ски, по-фран-цу́з-ски, по-и-та-лья́н-ски, по-я-по́н-ски

Б. Practice reading the phrases below aloud. Remember to use the proper intonation.

1. Кто[2] вы? Отку́да[2] вы?
2. Я студентка[1]. Я из России[1]. А вы[4]?
3. Мы читали[1] и говорили[1] по-ру́сски. А что вы де́лали[4]?
4. Её сестра́ студентка[3] и́ли школьница?
5. Мы зна́ем профессии[1]: преподаватель[1][3], писатель[3], журналист[3], переводчик[1]...

3. Что мы изуча́ли

Before you read.

1. Take <u>one minute</u> to scan through Part 1 (**Часть 1**) and say the names of the characters discussed in the text and where these people are from (in Russian).
2. Take <u>one minute</u> to scan through Part 2 (**Часть 2**) and say what professions are mentioned.

Часть 1

На́ша* те́ма — «Кто вы? Отку́да вы?» Мы чита́ли и говори́ли по-ру́сски. Мы изуча́ли грамма́тику, слу́шали диало́ги, чита́ли текст, де́лали упражне́ния, расска́зывали о себе́ по-ру́сски. *our

Тепе́рь мы зна́ем, что Ма́ша — студе́нтка из Росси́и, Юми — студе́нтка и певи́ца из Япо́нии, а То́мас — студе́нт и музыка́нт из Кана́ды.

А ещё* мы зна́ем, что* Ма́ша хорошо́ говори́т по-англи́йски. Её ма́ма — врач, а па́па — инжене́р. У Ма́ши есть брат. Его́ зову́т Ди́ма. Он — шко́льник. *also; *that

Юми и То́мас изуча́ют ру́сский язы́к в Росси́и. Они́ изуча́ют ру́сский то́лько оди́н год. Они́ хорошо́ чита́ют, но пло́хо понима́ют и ме́дленно говоря́т по-ру́сски.

Часть 2

Мы чита́ли тру́дные* слова́. Наприме́р*: расска́зывать и отдыха́ть. Мы зна́ем, что э́то глаго́лы*. А ещё мы зна́ем профе́ссии: преподава́тель, писа́тель, журнали́ст, перево́дчик... Это то́же* о́чень тру́дные слова́. *difficult; *for example *verbs *as well, also

Но не все* ру́сские слова́ тру́дные. Наприме́р, мы хорошо́ понима́ем слова́ ти́па* студе́нт, журнали́ст, профе́ссор, компози́тор, космона́вт, президе́нт. Не о́чень тру́дно чита́ть слова́ ти́па дом, кот, кни́га, уро́к, тест. *but not all *like, of this type

Мы непло́хо чита́ем по-ру́сски и немно́го понима́ем, когда́* говоря́т ме́дленно. Мы не понима́ем по-ру́сски, когда́ говоря́т бы́стро. *when

After you finish reading

Answer the following questions in Russian:

1) Кто Ма́ша? Отку́да она́? Кто по профе́ссии её ма́ма и па́па? Кто её брат?
2) Кто Юми? Кто То́мас? Что они́ де́лают в Росси́и? Как они́ чита́ют по-ру́сски? Как они́ понима́ют по-ру́сски? Как они́ говоря́т по-ру́сски?
3) Каки́е тру́дные слова́ мы чита́ли? Все ру́сские слова́ тру́дные? Каки́е слова́ не тру́дные?
4) Вы чита́ете по-ру́сски? Вы понима́ете по-ру́сски, когда́ говоря́т бы́стро?

4. Учим слова

Vocabulary building

1. Make a list of all professions mentioned in the above text.
2. Write out all verbs used from this text in their **infinitive** forms.

Flashcards

Make flashcards with words you want to know but have trouble remembering. Include the stress mark, the context, and the translation/image/explanation on the reverse side. Your flashcard should look similar to this:

Front side	*Reverse side*
шко́льник Мой брат – шко́льник.	
немно́го Я немно́го понима́ю по-ру́сски.	*a little bit*

- Whenever possible, draw a picture or write an explanation in Russian instead of the English translation on the reverse side.
- Memorize words in context.
- Carry your cards with you, and review them every day.
- Set aside the words you have memorized, but take them out again in a month to see if you still remember the words.

Чита́ем и понима́ем. Reading Russian folk tale "Ку́рочка Ря́ба" *Riaba the Hen*

Read the text aloud (You may choose to listen to the recording first.). Remember the pronunciation rules you have learned: reduction of unstressed vowels, consonant assimilation and devoicing of a final consonant.

Ку́рочка Ря́ба	***Riaba the Hen***
Ру́сская наро́дная ска́зка	***A Russian folk tale***
Жи́ли-бы́ли дед да ба́ба. И была́ у них ку́рочка Ря́ба.	*Once there lived an old man and an old woman. And they had a hen Riaba.*

Снесла́ ку́рочка яи́чко, да не просто́е, а золото́е.

The hen laid an egg, and not an ordinary one, but a golden one.

Дед бил, бил — не разби́л. Ба́ба би́ла, би́ла — не разби́ла.

The old man hit it and hit it, but could not break it. The old woman hit it and hit it, but could not break it.

Мы́шка бежа́ла, хво́стиком махну́ла, яи́чко упа́ло и разби́лось.

A mouse ran past, waved its tail, the egg fell and broke.

Дед пла́чет, ба́ба пла́чет, а ку́рочка куда́хчет: «Не плачь, дед, не плачь, ба́ба. Я снесу́ вам друго́е яи́чко, не золото́е — просто́е!»

The old man is crying, the old woman is crying, and the hen cackles: "Don't cry old man, don't cry old woman. I will lay you another egg, not a golden one, but an ordinary one!"

Коммента́рии

Жи́ли-бы́ли...

Жи́ли-бы́ли is the most common opening line in Russian folk tales. Literally it means "*there lived and existed*" (past tense from **жить** — *to live* and **быть** — *to be/exist*). The repetition of the two words, similar in their meaning, attunes the unhurried manner in which stories were told in the old times.

The word "да" used for "and"

The word **да** is sometimes used instead of **и** for "and':

... дед да ба́ба; да не просто́е, а золото́е

This is quite common in folk stories, proverbs, and sayings.

Verbs as sentence starters

One of the distinct features of a folk tale is the use of a verb as a sentence starter.

И была́ у них ку́рочка Ря́ба... Снесла́ ку́рочка яи́чко...

Normally, you would say: "У них была́ ку́рочка Ря́ба..." and "Ку́рочка снесла́ яи́чко."

Repetition

Another interesting feature of a folk tale is repetition of words that might seem unnecessary.

Дед бил, бил... Ба́ба би́ла, би́ла...

Дед пла́чет, ба́ба пла́чет... Не плачь, дед, не плачь, ба́ба...

This can also be seen as part of the original oral tradition of storytelling.

Diminutives

Diminutives are words used to convey various shades of meaning: from smallness of the object or quality named to endearment, tenderness, and intimacy. Russians frequently use diminutives when speaking to small children. In Russian folk tales, as well as in stories and poems for children, diminutives are used in abundance. Russian uses special suffixes to form diminutives. Study the examples of diminutives from our tale.

Ку́рочка (*dear little hen*) — derived from **ку́рица** (*hen*). The suffix-**очк**- forms the diminutive that conveys the meaning of endearment (old man and woman love their hen as it provides them with food).

Яи́чко (*little egg*) — derived from **яйцо́** (*egg*). Here we have the diminutive suffix -**ичк**-. It indicates that the egg is small and dear at the same time.

Мы́шка (*little mouse*) — derived from **мышь** (*mouse*) and **хво́стик** (*tiny/little tail*) — derived from **хвост** (*tail*) are formed with suffixes -**к**- and -**ик**-. The use of the diminutives for these words is very common due to the small size of both mouse and its tail.

Зада́ние 1. In the tale you have read, find and read aloud examples of:

a) words with unstressed, and therefore reduced, vowels о, е, and я, and

b) one word with a devoiced final consonant and one with consonant assimilation;

Зада́ние 2. This folk tale is one of the first Russian parents read to their kids. Can you tell what this simple story is about? How do you understand it? Discuss it with your instructor and classmates.

Тема 3
Какой вы человек? Что вы любите?

Практика

- **Како́й он? Кака́я она?** Describing people
- **Уче́бные предме́ты.** School subjects
- **Что вы лю́бите?** Likes and dislikes

Грамматика

- The plural form of nouns
- Noun and adjective agreement
- **Како́й? Как?** Adjectives vs. adverbs
- **Что?** What? vs. **Како́й?** What kind?
- Introduction to the case system. The nominative case of nouns and adjectives. The accusative case of nouns and adjectives
- Verb **люби́ть** — to love
- Verb **петь** — to sing

Культура

- Russia and the Russians

Читаем и понимаем

- Reading the lyrics "**Я полюби́ла Вас**" *I fell in love with you* by **Земфи́ра**

Акти́вный слова́рь. Те́ма 3

Nouns
Лю́ди — People
Кто?

граждани́н — *citizen*

друг — *friend (male)*

подру́га — *friend (female), girlfriend*

ребёнок — *child*

ребя́та — *kids, guys*

россия́нин — *Russian citizen (male)*

россия́нка — *Russian citizen (female)*

челове́к (лю́ди) — *person (people)*

Учё́бные предме́ты — School Subjects
Что?

антрополо́гия — *anthropology*

археоло́гия — *archeology*

архитекту́ра — *architecture*

биоло́гия — *biology*

ге́ндерные иссле́дования — *gender studies*

геоло́гия — *geology*

журнали́стика — *journalism*

информа́тика — *computer science*

искусствове́дение — *art studies*

компью́терная те́хника — *computer equipment*

лингви́стика — *linguistics*

литерату́ра — *literature*

матема́тика — *mathematics*

медици́на — *medicine*

междунаро́дные отноше́ния — *international relations*

музыкове́дение — *musicology, music history*

педаго́гика — *pedagogy*

политоло́гия — *Political Science*

психоло́гия — *psychology*

социоло́гия — *Social Science, sociology*

стати́стика — *statistics*

фи́зика — *physics*

филоло́гия — *philology*

филосо́фия — *philosophy*

фина́нсы — *finance*

хи́мия — *chemistry*

эконо́мика — *economy*

юриспруде́нция (правове́дение) — *jurisprudence, law*

Other Nouns
Что?

вечери́нка — *get-together party*

пе́сня — *song*

предме́т — *1) object; 2) school subject*

семе́стр — *semester, term*

университе́т — *university*

Verbs
Что де́лать?

петь (пою́, поёшь, пою́т) — *to sing*

расска́зывать (расска́зываю, расска́зываешь, расска́зывают) — *to tell*

Adjectives wih the opposite meaning
Како́й?

большо́й — *big, large*

ма́ленький — *little, small*

бы́стрый — *fast, quick*

ме́дленный — *slow*

дорого́й — *expensive; dear*

дешёвый — *cheap*

интере́сный — *it is interesting*

ску́чный — *boring*

но́вый — *new*

ста́рый — *old*

тру́дный — *difficult*

просто́й — *simple*

хоро́ший — *good*

плохо́й — *bad*

Other adjectives
Како́й?

акти́вный — *active*

америка́нский — *American*

ва́жный — *important*

до́брый — *kind, good*

кана́дский — *Canadian*

класси́ческий — *classical*

краси́вый — *beautiful*

люби́мый — *favorite*

междунаро́дный — *international*

опа́сный — *dangerous*

поле́зный — *useful*

популя́рный — *popular*

ра́зный — *different*

росси́йский — *Russian*

смешно́й — *funny*

сове́тский — *Soviet*

совреме́нный — *contemporary, modern*

тала́нтливый — *talented*

у́мный — *smart*

Урок 1

Это росси́йская певи́ца Земфи́ра.

Она́ у́мная и тала́нтливая. Она́ о́чень хорошо́ поёт.

Это англи́йский гитари́ст Джи́мми Пейдж.
Он у́мный и тала́нтливый.
Он о́чень хорошо́ игра́ет на гита́ре.

Како́й он? Кака́я она́? Describing people

Она́ тала́нтливая певи́ца.

Он тала́нтливый гита́рист.

Adjectives are used to describe people and objects. They answer the question "what kind of" person or thing. Adjectives change their endings to agree with nouns in gender, number and case. You will learn about adjective agreement later in this chapter. From now on, note the difference between masculine and feminine endings. The following adjectives are commonly used to describe people:

Он	**Она́**	
до́брый	до́брая	*kind*
весёлый	весёлая	*cheerful, happy*
у́мный	у́мная	*smart*
краси́вый	краси́вая	*beautiful*
интере́сный	интере́сная	*interesting*
ску́чный	ску́чная	*boring*
тала́нтливый	тала́нтливая	*talented*
серьёзный	серьёзная	*serious*
смешно́й	смешна́я	*funny*

When **не** is added to these adjectives, the new adjective has the opposite meaning: неинтере́сный — *not interesting*, некраси́вый — *not beautiful*, and so on.

Поговори́м! Let's talk!

3.1–1. Working with a partner, describe people and pets that you know. Use two or three adjectives from the above list in each description. Remember to use gender specific endings for adjectives.

Образе́ц: Моя́ ма́ма весёлая, до́брая и у́мная. А твоя́?

> **тво́й** — *yours (m.)*
> **твоя́** — *yours (f.)*

1. Моя́ мама ...
2. Мой па́па ...
3. Моя́ сестра́ ...
4. Мой брат ...
5. Мой друг ...
6. Моя́ подру́га ...
7. Моя́ соба́ка ...
8. Мой кот / моя́ ко́шка ...

> **подру́га** — *girlfriend or female friend*

Other common adjectives include:

но́вый	*new*	ста́рый	*old*
большо́й	*big*	ма́ленький	*small/little*
бы́стрый	*fast*	ме́дленный	*slow*
хоро́ший	*good*	плохо́й	*bad*
просто́й	*simple*	тру́дный	*difficult*
дорого́й	*expensive; dear*	дешёвый	*cheap*

ва́жный	*important*
люби́мый	*favourite*
поле́зный	*useful*
опа́сный	*dangerous*

3.1–2. Кака́я э́то профе́ссия?

A. In your notebook, write out the Russian adjectives that can be used to describe a profession. Pick from the list of common adjectives above and from the list of adjectives used to describe people.

Б. In your opinion, describe the professions listed below to your classmates. Use one or two adjectives to talk about each profession. You should use feminine forms of adjectives (replace the last two letters with **-ая** like this: поле́зн**ый** → поле́зн**ая**) to make them agree with the feminine noun **профе́ссия**.

Образе́ц: журнали́ст **Я ду́маю, что** журнали́ст — это **интере́сная профе́ссия**.

1. врач
2. инжене́р
3. писа́тель
4. бизнесме́н
5. учи́тель
6. космона́вт
7. компози́тор
8. бале́рина
9. актри́са
10. программи́ст

Я ду́маю, что — *I think that*

Жизнь в Росси́и: лю́ди, исто́рия, культу́ра
Russia and the Russians

Ру́сский vs. росси́йский

Russian language has two words for "Russian". One is **ру́сский** derived from the ancient name of the country **Русь** and refers to nationality, ethnic background.
The term **ру́сский** has to do with Russian culture, traditions, and Russian food and goes way beyond political borders. It is used in such word combinations as: ру́сский язы́к — *Russian language*, ру́сская культу́ра — *Russian culture*, ру́сская литерату́ра — *Russian literature*, ру́сские наро́дные пе́сни — *Russian folk songs*, ру́сские блины́ — *Russian pancakes*, ру́сская ба́ня — *Russian sauna*.

Росси́йский refers to the Russian state. This word originated in the 18th century when Peter the Great gave his state a new name **Росси́йская Импе́рия** — *The Russian Empire*. It was a state that existed from 1721 until the Russian Revolution of 1917.
The word росси́йский is commonly used in combinations like: росси́йский флаг — *Russian flag*, росси́йский па́спорт — *Russian passport*, росси́йская конститу́ция — *Russian constitution*, росси́йские спортсме́ны — *Russian athletes*.

After the October Revolution in 1917, Russia became part of the **СССР** (Сою́з Сове́тских Социалисти́ческих Респу́блик). Russia's official name between 1917 and 1991 was **РСФСР** (Росси́йская Сове́тская Федерати́вная Социалисти́ческая Респу́блика). The modern Russian state is officially called **Росси́йская Федера́ция** — *The Russian Federation* or **Росси́я** — *Russia*.

Ру́сский или россия́нин?

A person can be **ру́сский** by ethnic background living in or outside of the Russian state.
The term **россия́нин (россия́нка)** means *"a Russian citizen"*. **Россия́нин** is a person of Russian or a non-Russian ethnicity living in and being a citizen of the Russian Federation — **росси́йский граждани́н**.

Читáйте текст. Мои́ нóвые друзья́

У меня́ есть нóвые друзья́* — Тóмас из Канáды и Юми из Япóнии. Мы познакóмились мéсяц* назáд*. Мой нóвый друг Тóмас — óчень интерéсный человéк*. Он ýмный, дóбрый и весёлый. А ещё Тóмас талáнтливый музыкáнт.

*friends
*month; *ago
*person

Моя́ нóвая подрýга Юми краси́вая, ýмная и серьёзная. Онá талáнтливая певи́ца и óчень хорóшая студéнтка.

Вопрóсы

1. Как вы дýмаете, кто э́то расскáзывает*?
   а) Мáша;
   б) её брат Ди́ма;
   в) Анна Алексáндровна
2. Когдá они́ познакóмились?
3. Какóй человéк Тóмас? Расскажи́те.
4. Какóй человéк Юми? Расскажи́те.

*tells

Расскажи́те — *Tell us; Tell me*

Слýшайте и читáйте диалóги.

1. Это твоя́ сестрá?

Мáша: Это твоя́ сестрá?
Юми: Да, э́то моя́ сестрá.
Мáша: Навéрное*, онá óчень серьёзная.
Юми: Нет, э́то прóсто* такáя фотогрáфия. Асáми весёлая и смешнáя.

*probably
*just

2. Это твоя́ кóшка?

Тóмас: Это твоя́ кóшка?
Мáша: Да, э́то моя́ кóшка. Её зовýт Мýрка.
Тóмас: Какáя смéшная! А что онá лю́бит* дéлать?

to love, like (all forms are listed in Урок 6 of Тема 3)

Ма́ша: Му́рка лю́бит игра́ть. Она́ о́чень акти́вная и весёлая ко́шка.

То́мас: А кто э́то?

Ма́ша: Это Земфи́ра. Моя́ люби́мая росси́йская певи́ца.

То́мас: Интере́сно! А каки́е пе́сни она́ поёт*? — *sings

Ма́ша: Ра́зные*. В основно́м* рок и блюз. А что ты лю́бишь слу́шать? — *different *above all

То́мас: Я люблю́ слу́шать класси́ческий рок. Мой люби́мый музыка́нт Джи́мми Пейдж. Это о́чень тала́нтливый гитари́ст. Он кла́ссно* игра́ет! — *awesome

3. Хоро́шие друзья́

Анна Алекса́ндровна: Хоро́шие друзья́ у Ма́ши, пра́вда?

Ива́н Петро́вич: Да! Очень хоро́шие. Серьёзные и у́мные ребя́та.

Анна Алекса́ндровна: И тала́нтливые музыка́нты.

Ива́н Петро́вич: А отку́да ты зна́ешь, что они́ тала́нтливые?

> **А отку́да ты зна́ешь —** *How do you know?*

Анна Алекса́ндровна: Ма́ша сказа́ла, что То́мас игра́ет на гита́ре, а Юми краси́во поёт.

Ива́н Петро́вич: Ну, э́то Ма́ша сказа́ла... А я не слы́шал их и не зна́ю тала́нтливые они́ и́ли нет.

Анна Алекса́ндровна: Я ду́маю, что Ма́ша зна́ет, что говори́т.

Ива́н Петро́вич: Ну, хорошо́, хорошо́. Я не спо́рю*. — *argue

3.1–3. Вопро́сы к диало́гам. Answer the following questions based on what you learned in the dialogues above.

1. Кака́я сестра́ Юми? Расскажи́те.
2. Кака́я ко́шка у Ма́ши? Что она́ лю́бит де́лать?
3. Кто така́я Земфи́ра? Каки́е пе́сни она́ поёт?
4. Что ду́мает Анна Алекса́ндровна о друзья́х Ма́ши?
5. Почему́ Анна Алекса́ндровна ду́мает, что они́ тала́нтливые?
6. Что говори́т Ива́н Петро́вич о друзья́х Ма́ши?

Кто тако́й? Кто така́я? — *Who is this (person)?*

ваш, ва́ша — *yours (formal)*

3.1–4. Расскажи́те о ва́ших друзья́х. Tell about your friends.

Как его́/её зову́т? Отку́да он/она́? Кто он/она́ по профе́ссии?
Како́й ваш друг? Кака́я ва́ша подру́га?
Начни́те так (*Begin like this*):
У меня́ есть хоро́ший друг. Его́ зову́т ... / У меня́ есть хоро́шая подру́га. Её зову́т ...

3.1–5. Try to imagine yourself in about 10 years from now. What kind of person are you? How do you look? What do you do? Use the vocabulary introduced in this chapter to tell your classmates about your imagined future self. Consult with your teacher or refer to a dictionary for more descriptive words.

Поговори́м! Let's talk!

3.1–6. Bring a picture of your friend/relative/pet and prepare words and phrases to talk about him/her. Working with a partner, discuss your pictures. Use vocabulary and phrases introduced in this and previous chapters.

- Say the person's/ pet's name.
- Describe his/her personality and appearance.
- Describe his/her occupation and what do you think about this profession (интере́сная, тру́дная, etc.)
- Describe what he/she loves to do.

Поговори́м! Let's talk!

3.1–7. With a partner, create a dialogue discussing a person from the images below. Imagine that one of you knows that person. The one of you who does not know that person asks questions. In your dialogue, you should mention:

- the person's name and relation to one of you (друг, подру́га, брат, сестра́, дя́дя, тётя, etc.),
- his/her personality and appearance,
- his/her occupation, and
- his/her likes and dislikes (Что он/она́ лю́бит де́лать? Что он/она́ не лю́бит де́лать?).

Memorize your dialogue, and act it out for the rest of the class.

Это ____________________

Это ____________________

Это ____________________

Это ____________________

Это ____________________

Это ____________________

Урок 2

The Plural Form of Nouns

Regular Forms

When a word refers to more than one person or thing, it is called **plural**. Russian nouns form the plural by changing the ending. Typically, masculine and feminine nouns take-**ы** or-**и** in the plural. Neuter nouns take-**а** or-**я** in the plural.

	Masculine	Feminine	Neuter
Hard Stem	журна́л → журна́л**ы**	газе́т**а** → газе́т**ы**	сло́в**о** → слов**а́**
Soft Stem	музе́**й** → музе́**и** слова́р**ь** → словар**и́**	стать**я́** → стать**и́** тетра́д**ь** → тетра́д**и**	пла́ть**е** → пла́ть**я**
Plural endings	**-ы/-и**		**-а/-я**

- For the feminine and neuter nouns, remember to remove the singular ending (the last vowel letter-а,-я,-о,-е, the final-ь or-й) before adding plural ending. Do not remove the final consonant from a masculine noun.
- Only remove the **ь** if it is the very last letter in a word like in словарь, words like статья or платье keep their **ь** as it is not the ending.
- Hard stem nouns take "hard" endings:-**ы** (masculine and feminine) or-**а** (neuter). Soft stem nouns take "soft" endings:-**и** (masculine and feminine) or-**я** (neuter). Review Урок 4 in the introductory chapter for details about hard and soft consonants.
- The stress can shift in the plural like in слова́р**ь** → словар**и́** or сло́в**о** → слов**а́**. Such changes are marked in dictionaries and have to be memorized.

3.2–1. Form the regular plural of the following nouns. All these nouns have stable stress. (It does not change in the plural.) Can you say what each word means?

студе́нт
преподава́тель
профе́ссия
космона́вт
инжене́р
актри́са
балери́на

пра́вило
упражне́ние
вопро́с
отве́т
страни́ца
тетра́дь
перево́д

- **The 7-letter spelling rule**

  After letters **к**, **г**, **х** and **ж**, **ш**, **ч**, **щ**, never write **ы**, write **и** instead.

  уче́бник → уче́бники   врач → врачи́

  кни́га → кни́ги   каранда́ш → карандаши́

  ~~ы~~

ки	жи
ги	ши
хи	чи
	щи

3.2–2. Choose the correct letter (either **ы** or **и**) for the plural ending of nouns listed below. Explain your answer. Do you remember what each word means?

ру́чка

каранда́ш *(stress moves to ending)*

журна́л

газе́та

уро́к

текст

плащ *(stress moves to ending)*

оши́бка

нож *(stress moves to ending)*

ча́шка

ча́йник

кни́га

певи́ца

язы́к *(stress moves to ending)*

- **Masculine nouns with -á in the plural**

  Some masculine nouns take stressed-**á** (rarely-**я́**) in the plural. Dictionaries provide the plural for such nouns. From this chapter, you should learn five such nouns:

  дом → дома́

  го́род → города́

  па́спорт → паспорта́

  профе́ссор → профессора́

  учи́тель → учителя́

- **No change in the plural**

  Certain nouns of *foreign origin* never change. They are called *indeclinable* nouns. Such nouns typically end in -**о**, -**е**, -**и**, rarely -**у** and are easy to recognize for an English speaker. Their plural is the same as singular:

ра́дио	ко́фе	кенгуру́
метро́	такси́	пиани́но
пальто́*		

- **Plural different from singular**

  Some nouns look quite different in the plural (like English child → children). Their plural forms must be memorized:

друг → друзья́	*friend — friends*
челове́к → лю́ди	*person — people*
ребёнок → де́ти	*child — children*

3.2–3. Put the following nouns in the plural. Here you will have a mix of regular plural forms, words that are subject to 7-letter spelling rule, and exceptions. Explain your choice of ending.

актёр	шко́льник	го́род
актри́са	писа́тель	дом
журнали́ст	профе́ссор	метро́
спортсме́н	учи́тель	перево́д
спортсме́нка	друг	предложе́ние
бизнесме́н	компози́тор	диало́г
врач *(stress moves to ending)*	перево́дчик	письмо́ *(stress moves to front u)*
гимна́стка	музыка́нт	

* The word **пальто́** — *long warm overcoat* is borrowed from French (*paletot*). Most indeclinable loan words are either English or French origin.

Урок 3

Noun and Adjective Agreement

Adjectives in the Nominative Case
Regular Forms

Russian adjectives change their ending to agree in gender, number, and case with the noun they modify.

In the Nominative case, each adjective has four different forms: masculine, feminine, neuter, and plural.

Masculine	интере́сн**ый** журна́л	-ый
Feminine	интере́сн**ая** кни́га	-ая
Neuter	интере́сн**ое** письмо́	-ое
Plural	интере́сн**ые** журна́лы	-ые
	кни́ги	
	пи́сьма	

- Dictionaries and word lists introduce adjectives in their masculine form. You can turn the masculine adjective into feminine, neuter, or plural by changing its ending.
- Adjectives have a two-letter ending. To change the adjective agreement, remove the two final letters from the masculine form before adding the appropriate ending: интере́сн-**ый** → интере́сн-**ая**.

3.3–1. Describe the following objects as "new" in Russian. Remember to use proper adjective ending.

Уче́бник, маши́на, дом, гита́ра, пиани́но, тетра́ди, слова́рь, письмо́, ру́чка, каранда́ш, пальто́, друг, подру́га, друзья́.

Образе́ц: но́в**ый** уче́бник

- **Masculine adjectives with -о́й ending**

  Some masculine adjectives have stressed-**о́й** ending in the Nominative case:
  This does not affect other forms. They remain regular:

больш**о́й**	*big*	больш**о́й**, больш**а́я**, больш**о́е**, больш**и́е**
плох**о́й**	*bad*	плох**о́й**, плох**а́я**, плох**о́е**, плох**и́е**
прост**о́й**	*simple*	прост**о́й**, прост**а́я**, прост**о́е**, прост**ы́е**
смешн**о́й**	*funny*	смешн**о́й**, смешн**а́я**, смешн**о́е**, смешн**ы́е**

  Note that these adjectives keep the end stress in all forms!

- **The 7-letter spelling rule**

  This rule is universal in Russian language. After letters **к**, **г**, **х** and **ж**, **ш**, **ч**, **щ**, never write **ы**; write **и** instead. You have to keep these 7 letters in mind when dealing with masculine and plural endings:

masculine:	ру́сский, ма́ленький, хоро́ший
plural:	ру́сские, ма́ленькие, хоро́шие, больши́е, плохи́е

ки	жи
ги	ши
хи	чи
ы	щи

3.3–2. А. Describe the following professionals as "good" in Russian. Remember to use the proper adjective ending. Add a personal pronoun он, она or они to make a sentence.

Образец: Он хоро́ш**ий** врач.

Врач, актёр, певе́ц, певи́ца, спортсме́ны, врачи́, инжене́ры, переводчи́к, учителя́, преподава́тели.

Б. Now say that these professionals are "bad" in Russian?

Образец: Он плох**о́й** врач.

- **The 5-letter spelling rule**

  This rule applies only to adjectives with unstressed endings. It affects the spelling of neuter endings of adjectives in the Nominative case.

  After the hushing consonants **ж**, **ш**, **ч**, **щ** and the consonant **ц**, write **е** if the ending is not stressed. If the ending is stressed, write regular **о** in the ending. For example, the word большóй has the letter **ш** before the stressed ending, and its neuter form is больш**óе**. The word хорóший has the letter **ш** before unstressed ending, and its neuter form is хорóш**ее**.

  m. больш**óй** → n. больш**óе** stressed neuter ending after **ш**

  m. хорóш**ий** → n. хорóш**ее** unstressed neuter ending after **ш**

  Not many adjectives are subject to this rule. In this chapter, you will only learn one word with neuter-**ее** at the end: хорóш**ий** → хорóш**ее**.

- **Adjectives with soft -н-**

  Some adjectives have soft-**н**- stem. If dictionary form of an adjective ends in-**ний**, its ending is soft in all other forms:-**няя**,-**нее**,-**ние**. So far you have seen one such adjective:

  m. домáш**ний**, f. домáш**няя**, n. домáш**нее**, pl. домáш**ние** (*home*)

  Note that many adjectives have hard -**ный** at the end (трýдный, полéзный, вáжный). They have regular hard endings:-ный,-ная,-ное,-ные.

3.3–3. Take out three objects from your bag, find out from your instructor or look up in the dictionary what they are in Russian if you don't know. Describe these objects using the adjectives from the list below. Use at least two adjectives to describe each object. Remember to use the proper adjective endings depending on the gender and number of the noun. Write down your sentences.

Нóвый, стáрый, большóй, мáленький, хорóший, плохóй, дорогóй, дешёвый, опáсный, вáжный, полéзный, интерéсный.

Образéц: Это интерéсная рýсская кни́га.

Поговори́м! Let's talk!

3.3–4. With a partner, discuss the things you each took out from your bag and described in the exercise 3.3-3. Point to one of your partner's objects and ask Что это? and Како́й/Кака́я/Како́е/Каки́е э́то ...? questions to create a conversation similar to the model below.

Образе́ц:

— Что э́то?
— Это слова́рь.
— Како́й э́то слова́рь?
— Это но́вый ру́сский слова́рь.

The question word **Како́й** (*What kind?*) is an adjective and has four different forms: Как**о́й**? Как**а́я**? Как**о́е**? Как**и́е**?

3.3–5. Disagree with the following statements by using adjectives with the opposite meaning.

Образе́ц: Это **большо́й** го́род. — А я ду́маю, что **ма́ленький**.

1. Это мале́нький дом.
2. Это интере́сная статья́.
3. Это дорого́й учёбник.
4. Это просто́е пра́вило.
5. Это но́вый компью́тер.
6. Это хоро́шая пе́сня.
7. Это хоро́ший перево́д.
8. Это смешно́й расска́з.
9. Это тру́дное упражне́ние.
10. Это краси́вые пла́тья.

Урок 4

Какóй? Как? Adjectives vs. Adverbs

Adjectives describe nouns (people, things, concepts, etc.) and change their endings to agree with that noun. Adjectives answer the question *What kind? — Какой?*

— Какóй он студéнт?	— *What kind of student he is?*
— Он **хорóший** студéнт.	— *He is a **good** student.*
— Какóй э́то дом?	— *What kind of house is this?*
— Это **нóвый** дом.	— *It's a **new** house.*

Adverbs describe verbs (actions), and also adjectives and other adverbs. Adverbs do not change: they do not have gender or number. They answer question *How? — Как?*

— Как студéнт читáет?	— *How does the student read?*
— Он **хорошó** читáет.	— *He reads **well**.*
— Как студéнты читáют?	— *How do the students read?*
— Они́ **хорошó** читáют.	— *They read **well**.*

Some other questions that adverbs can answer include: *how much? — сколько?*; *when? — когда?*; and *where? — где?*

- Many adverbs are derived from adjectives. Such adverbs typically have **-о**, **-ски**, **-ому** at the end:

хорóший → хорош**ó**	англи́йский → по-англи́й**ски**
бы́стрый → бы́стр**о**	рýсский → по-рýс**ски**
интерéсный → интерéсн**о**	нóвый → по-нóв**ому**

- Some adverbs are not related to any adjective. For example: там (*there*), о́чень (*very*), пото́м (*then*), сейча́с (*now*).
- In English, adjectives and adverbs may look exactly the same. In Russian, adjectives and adverbs always have their specific endings. Compare:

*This is a **fast** program.*	Это **бы́страя** програ́мма.
*It works **fast**.*	Она́ рабо́тает **бы́стро**.
Adjective and adverb look the same.	*Adjective and adverb differ at the end.*

To avoid confusion when translating such words into Russian, remember that adjectives modify nouns and pronouns, while adverbs modify verbs, adjectives, and other adverbs.

3.4–1. Adjective or adverb? Look at the English sentences below and translate the italicized words with an adjective or adverb. Explain your choice.

Образе́ц: This is an *interesting* book. (интере́сная, интере́сно)

The adjective **интере́сная** must be used because it modifies the noun 'book'.

1. The train goes *fast*. (бы́стрый, бы́стро)
2. This is a *slow* car. (ме́дленная, ме́дленно)
3. The essay is very *well* written. (хоро́шее, хорошо́)
4. This is a very *good* essay. (хоро́шее, хорошо́)
5. She is walking *slowly*. (ме́дленная, ме́дленно)
6. She a *beautiful* girl. (краси́вая, краси́во)
7. She looks *beautiful* today. (краси́вая, краси́во)
8. I have a *Russian* friend. (ру́сский, по-ру́сски)
9. He speaks *Russian*. (ру́сский, по-ру́сски)
10. I love *Russian* language. (ру́сский, по-ру́сски)

3.4–2. Complete the sentences with adjectives or adverbs in parenthesis.

Образе́ц: Моя́ сестра́ о́чень **краси́во** поёт. (краси́вая, краси́во)

1. Как он чита́ет ____________? (ру́сский, по-ру́сски)
2. Он чита́ет ____________. (ме́дленный, ме́дленно)

3. Ма́ша __________ зна́ет англи́йский язы́к. (хоро́шая, хорошо́)
4. Она́ __________ певи́ца. (тала́нтливая, тала́нтливо)
5. Извини́те, я __________ понима́ю по-ру́сски. (плохо́й, пло́хо)
6. Он __________ расска́зывает. (интере́сный, интере́сно)
7. Он __________ челове́к. (весёлый, ве́село)
8. Это __________ кни́га. (ску́чная, ску́чно)

Поговори́м! Let's talk!

3.4–3. In a group of three or four, discuss a singer, a musician, or an actor/actress. Describe the person with at least two adjectives and use an adverb to comment on how he/she sings/plays/acts. You can bring a picture of that person to show to your classmates.

- Verbs to review:

  Он / Она́ поёт. — *He/she sings.*

  Он / Она́ игра́ет (You may add an instrument like this: на гитаре, на пианино.). — *He/she plays...*

  Он / Она́ игра́ет. — *He/she acts.*

- While one student is talking, others should participate by making comments like:

  Я его / её зна́ю!

  Да, он о́чень хоро́ший актёр! or Нет, я ду́маю, что он плохо́й актёр.

  Интере́сно!

  Try to create your own comments based on vocabulary and sentence structures familiar to you.

Что? What? vs. Како́й? What Kind?

The question *Что?* means *What?* Note that there is no noun in a *Что-question* itself. A noun, pronoun or a verb is used to answer *Что-question*:

— Что э́то? — *What is that?*

— Это **журна́л**. — *That is a **magazine**.*

— Что ты де́лаешь? — *What are you doing?*

— Я **чита́ю**. — *I'm **reading**.*

— Что ты чита́ешь?	— *What are you reading?*
— Я чита́ю **журна́л**.	— *I'm reading a **magazine**.*

The question word *Какой?* means *What kind?* Note that there is always a noun in *Какой-question*. An adjective is typically used to answer it:

— Како́й э́то журна́л?	— *What (kind of) magazine is that?*
— Это **совреме́нный ру́сский** журна́л.	— *This is a **modern Russian** magazine.*

Како́й changes its endings for gender, number, and case to agree with the noun in question.

— Кака́я э́то кни́га?	— *What (kind of) book is that?*
— Это **интере́сная ру́сская** кни́га.	— *This is an **interesting Russian** book.*
— Како́е э́то пра́вило?	— *What (kind of) rule is that?*
— Это **тру́дное** пра́вило.	— *This is a **difficult** rule.*
— Каки́е э́то студе́нты?	— *What (kind of) students are they?*
— Это **хоро́шие** студе́нты.	— *They are **good** students.*

Translation tips

English often omits the "kind of" part of the question: *What book is that? = What kind of book is that?*
When translating *what* into Russian watch for a noun in the question:

- If there is a noun in the question, *what* is adjectival and a form of *како́й* must be used:

  What book is that? Кака́я э́то кни́га?

  The noun "book" is used in the question → Translate *what* as *Как**ая*** because кни́г**а** is a feminine noun.

  What journal are you reading? Како́й журна́л ты чита́ешь?

  The noun "journal" is used in the question → Translate *what* as *Как**ой*** because журна́л is a masculine noun.

- If there is no noun in the question, translate *what* as *что*:

What is that?	Что э́то?
What are you reading?	Что ты чита́ешь?

No noun is used in these questions → Translate *what* as *что*.

- If you can replace *what* with *what kind* without changing the meaning of the question, it is a form of ***како́й***, if not, it is ***что***. Compare:

  What journal are you reading? = What kind of journal are you reading? → translate *what* as ***како́й...***?

  What are you reading? ≠ "What kind of are you reading?" (The second question does not make sense.) → translate *what* as ***что...***?

3.4–4. Что or **Како́й? Кака́я? Како́е? Каки́е?** Fill in the blanks with the correct Russian question word.

1. What do you study? ______________ ты изуча́ешь?
2. What language do you study? ______________ язы́к ты изуча́ешь?
3. What books do you like? ______________ кни́ги ты лю́бишь?
4. What are you listening to? ______________ ты слу́шаешь?
5. What music is that? ______________ э́то му́зыка?
6. What is that? ______________ э́то?

3.4–5. Translate the dialogue into Russian.

— What are you reading?

— A journal.

— What journal?

— It's an old Russian journal. I read slowly.

— Do you know this word?

— Which word?

— Do you know the word «учебник»?

— Yes, in Russian it's "textbook"?

Урок 5

Introduction to the Case System

The system of putting endings on nouns, pronouns, and adjectives to show their role in a sentence is called a **Case System**.
English, for example, has the ending -s added to a noun to show ownership (called the **possessive case**):

*This is my **dad's** guitar.*

English pronouns change to reflect their function in a sentence:

***She** knows **him**. **He** knows **her**.*

You cannot say "She knows *he*" or "He knows *she*" because the forms *he* and *she* cannot be used as objects of a verb. They indicate a subject.

In English, however, there are only few instances in which a noun changes ending as it assumes a new role in a sentence. The word order usually helps you recognize the function of the nouns and their meaning in the entire sentence. Compare these two English sentences:

Father gave **the boy** an apple.	**The boy** gave **father** an apple.
Father is giving and the boy is receiving it.	*The boy is giving and father is receiving it.*

The word order in these sentences tells you who is giving and who is receiving an apple.

In Russian, word order alone does not usually show the function of a noun in a sentence. Different endings of a noun correspond to its various functions creating a rich case system. There are six cases in Russian: nominative, genitive, dative, accusative, prepositional, and instrumental. Each case and its functions will be introduced gradually. In this chapter, you will learn forms and main functions of the Nominative and the Accusative cases.

The Nominative Case

Nouns, pronouns, and adjectives in dictionaries and word lists are given in the Nominative case. This is their basic form. In a sentence, the Nominative case is used for:

- The subject of the sentence.

<u>То́мас</u> студе́нт. Subject	*<u>Thomas</u> is a student.* Subject

- The predicate complement words in a sentence (where "to be" is the understood verb).

Тóмас студéнт. — *Thomas is a student.*
(студéнт: Predicate complement) — (*student*: Predicate complement)

Nominative Case Overview

Let's review the basic facts you have learned about the Nominative case forms.

- Russian nouns belong to three different genders. We can tell the noun's gender by looking at its nominative case ending:

masculine	журнáл
feminine	газéт**а**
neuter	письм**ó**

- To form the nominative plural of noun we change its ending:

plural	журнáл**ы**
	газéт**ы**
	пи́сьм**а**

- Adjectives always agree with the noun they modify. As a result, they have four different forms in the Nominative case:

masculine	интерéсн**ый** журнáл
feminine	интерéсн**ая** газéт**а**
neuter	интерéсн**ое** письм**ó**
plural	интерéсн**ые** журнáл**ы**, газéт**ы**, пи́сьм**а**

Читáйте тéкст. Интерéсные кни́ги, газéты, журнáлы.

Read the text below, and find examples of

а) nouns and adjectives in the nominative singular and

б) nouns and adjectives in the nominative plural.

Я люблю́ читáть. У меня́ есть интерéсные кни́ги, газéты, журнáлы.

ПРАВДА
Орган Центрального Комитета КПСС
Родом из Октября
ПРАЗДНИЧНЫЙ ПРИЕМ в Кремлевском Дворце съездов

Вот «Пра́вда» — ста́рая сове́тская* газе́та. Тут «Афи́ша» — совреме́нный* росси́йский журна́л о кино́. А э́то мои́ ру́сские и англи́йские кни́ги: «Анна Каре́нина», «Ма́стер и Марга́рита», «Оливер Твист», «Хо́ббит».

*soviet
*contemporary,

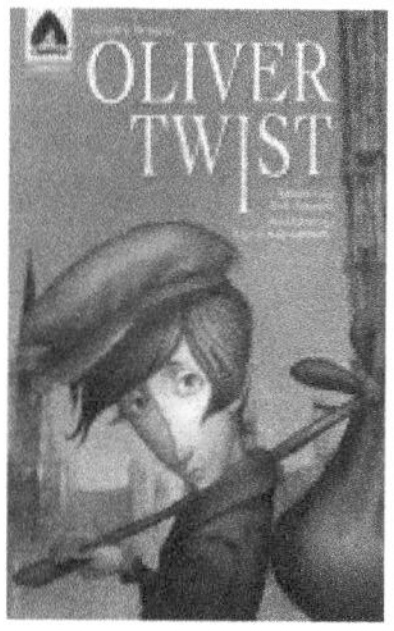

Вопро́сы

1) У вас есть кни́ги? Каки́е э́то кни́ги?
2) У вас есть газе́ты и журна́лы? Они́ ску́чные и́ли интере́сные? Они́ ста́рые и́ли совреме́нные?

The Accusative Case

Some sentences consist of only a subject and a verb:

<u>Ма́ша</u> чита́ет.	*Masha is reading.*
Subject Verb	Subject Verb

A subject can be more complex:

<u>Ру́сская студе́нтка Ма́ша</u> чита́ет.	*<u>Russian student Masha</u> is reading.*
Subject Verb	Subject Verb

The **nominative case** of a noun and its modifiers is used to indicate the subject of a sentence. Many sentences, however, contain other nouns and pronouns that often function as objects of verbs.

To indicate a **direct object** of the verb, the **accusative case** is used. The direct object is a noun or a pronoun that receives the action of the verb directly, without intervening prepositions. It answers the question Кого? (*Whom?*) or Что? (*What?*) Study the following sentences:

Ма́ша лю́бит ма́му. — *Masha loves mom.*

Subject — Direct object of the verb

Masha loves *whom?* Answer: *mom.*

Ма́ша чита́ет интере́сную кни́гу. — *Masha is reading an interesting book.*

Subject — Direct object of the verb

Masha reads *what?* Answer: *an interesting book.*

Accusative case is also used for objects of certain prepositions. You will learn more about accusative case use as you progress.

Чита́йте те́кст. Кто что чита́ет? Расска́зывает ру́сская студе́нтка Ма́ша.

Read the text and identify all direct objects used here. Underline them.

> You have seen two words for 'also': **тоже** and **также**.
>
> Use **тоже** when two different subjects do the same thing:
> Юми изучает русский язык. Томас тоже изучает русский язык.
>
> Use **также** when one subject does two different things:
> Юми часто читает газеты, а также новости в Интернете.
>
> You will learn more about тоже and также in Тема 5 (Part 2).

Я люблю́ чита́ть. Я чита́ю ра́зные* газе́ты, журна́лы, кни́ги. — **different*

Неда́вно* я чита́ла но́вый англи́йский рома́н, а сейча́с* чита́ю интере́сную ру́сскую кни́гу. — **recently; *now*

Мой кана́дский друг То́мас лю́бит чита́ть «Афи́шу». Это совреме́нный ру́сский журна́л о кино́. Моя́ подру́га из Япо́нии Юми ча́сто* чита́ет газе́ты, а та́кже ново́сти* в Интерне́те. — **often; *news (pl.)*

А ещё мы лю́бим слу́шать музы́ку. Я слу́шаю блюз и рок, То́мас слу́шает джаз, а Юми слу́шает популя́рную и класси́ческую му́зыку.

Вопро́сы

Some nouns and adjectives change their endings for the accusative case and some don't. Can you tell which nouns change for the accusative case and what endings they take? What is the gender of these nouns?

Accusative Case of Nouns and Adjectives
Regular forms

The following chart shows the accusative case forms of nouns and adjectives.

Gender, Number	Nominative case forms	Accusative case forms
Masculine	интере́сн**ый** журна́л	интере́сн**ый** журна́л
Neuter	интере́сн**ое** письм**о́**	интере́сн**ое** письм**о́**
Feminine	интере́сн**ая** кни́г**а**	интере́сн**ую** кни́г**у**
Plural	интере́сн**ые** журна́л**ы** кни́г**и** пи́сьм**а**	интере́сн**ые** журна́л**ы** кни́г**и** пи́сьм**а**

- Feminine phrases (nouns and their modifiers) change for the accusative case. Apply these simple rules to form accusative feminine:

-а → **-у**	кни́г**а** → кни́г**у**, ма́м**а** → ма́м**у**
-я → **-ю**	ста́ть**я** → ста́ть**ю**, исто́ри**я** → исто́ри**ю**
-ь → no change	тетрад**ь** → тетра́д**ь**

Adjectives always have two letter endings; replace both letters to form the accusative feminine:

-ая → **-ую**	интере́сн**ая** → интере́сн**ую**
-яя → **-юю**	дома́шн**яя** → дома́шн**юю**

Ма́ша чита́ет но́в**ую** кни́г**у**. Юми чита́ет интере́сн**ую** стать**ю́**.

Тóмас читáет стáрую тетрáдь. Дúма дéлает домáшнюю рабóту.

- Neuter phrases never change for the accusative case:

  Мáша читáет интерéсное письмó.

- Masculine and plural inanimate phrases never change for the accusative case:

  Маша читáла нóвый англúйский ромáн.

- Masculine and plural animate phrases take genitive case endings in the accusative case:

  Мáша знáет канáдск**ого** студéнт**а** Тóмас**а**.

  You will study the genitive case endings later. For now, consult your teacher if you are trying to use animate masculine and plural phrases in the accusative case.

- Как**áя** → Какýю ... The feminine form of the question word what/what kind changes like an adjective for the accusative case:

  Какýю мýзыку слýшает Тóмас?

Exceptions

- Masculine nouns ending in **-а/-я** (**пáпа**, **дéдушка**, **дя́дя**, **Дúма**, etc.) change like feminine nouns regardless the fact that they refer to male persons:

  Я люблю́ папу и дéдушку. Я хорошó знáю Дúму.

3.5–1. Кто что читáет? Complete the sentences with the correct accusative forms of words and phrases in parenthesis.

1. Ивáн Петрóвич читáет ______________________ (газéта).
2. Анна Петрóвна читáет ______________________ (нóвый ромáн).
3. Мáша читáет ______________________ (стáрый скýчный учéбник).
4. Дúма читáет ______________________ (смешнáя скáзка).
5. Юми читáет ______________________ (серьёзная статья́).
6. Тóмас читáет ______________________ (трýдное рýсское слóво).
7. Бáбушка читáет ______________________ (письмó).
8. Я читáю ______________________ (рýсская кнúга).
9. Студéнты читáют ______________________ (нóвые диалóги).
10. Преподавáтель читáет ______________________ (трýдное предложéние).

Уче́бные предме́ты. School Subjects

— Что вы изуча́ете?

— Я изуча́ю ру́сскую литерату́ру и исто́рию.

The majority of words for school subjects in Russian are feminine nouns with-**а** or-**ия** ending. You will easily understand their meanings, as most of them are international words.
When talking about courses that you take, use the structure: **Я изуча́ю** (*I study*) + the school subject in the accusative case. The Russian verb for "take" is not used for "taking courses".
Study the list of subjects and give their English equivalents:

Читайте вслух. Read aloud.

антрополо́гия
англи́йский язы́к
археоло́гия
архитекту́ра
биоло́гия
геоло́гия
геогра́фия
журнали́стика
информа́тика и компью́терная те́хника
исто́рия
лингви́стика
литерату́ра
матема́тика
медици́на

му́зыка
педаго́гика
политоло́гия
психоло́гия
ру́сский язы́к
стати́стика
социоло́гия
фи́зика
филоло́гия
филосо́фия
фина́нсы
францу́зский язы́к
хи́мия
эконо́мика

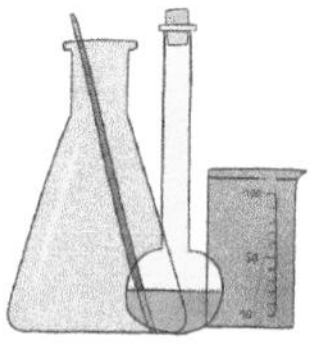

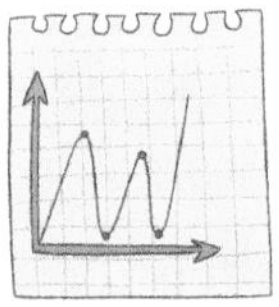

The meaning of the following terms may not be as obvious for an English speaker. Read them aloud to master their pronunciations:

Читайте вслух. Read aloud.

ге́ндерные иссле́дования	*gender studies*
искусствове́дение	*art history*
музыкове́дение	*music history, musicology*
междунаро́дные отноше́ния	*international relations*
междунаро́дное пра́во	*international law*
юриспруде́нция (правове́дение)	*law, jurisprudence*

3.5–2. Что вы изуча́ете? Tell us which subjects/courses from the above lists you are taking: **(Я изуча́ю)** and which ones you want to take: **(Я хочу́ изуча́ть)**. Remember to use the correct accusative endings for subjects.

Я хочу́ — *I want to*

Поговори́м! Let's talk!

3.5–3. With a partner take turns asking and answering questions about the subjects from the list above. Find out if your partner is taking any of these subjects.

Образе́ц:

— Ты изуча́ешь искусствове́дение?
— Да, изуча́ю./Нет, не изуча́ю. А ты?

3.5–4. Make meaningful sentences from the elements below. You should use all four elements to create the structure: Subject + Verb + (Adjective + Noun).

Direct Object

Each word is given in its basic dictionary form. Change endings where necessary.

Образе́ц: Ба́бушка расска́зыва**ет** интере́сн**ую** исто́ри**ю**.

Grammatical Subject	Verb	Adjective	Object noun
ба́бушка	чита́ть	но́вый	кни́га
ма́ма	понима́ть	ста́рый	газе́та
па́па	расска́зывать	ру́сский	журна́л
студе́нты	изуча́ть	англи́йский	письмо́

Grammatical Subject	Verb	Adjective	Object noun
мой друг	слу́шать	класси́ческий	слова́рь
моя́ подру́га	по́мнить	просто́й	тетра́дь
я	знать	тру́дный	архитекту́ра
мы	де́лать	интере́сный	исто́рия
они́	писа́ть	ску́чный	литерату́ра
де́ти		весёлый	но́вости
преподава́тель		серьёзный	статья́
		смешно́й	диало́г
		дома́шний	упражне́ние
		хоро́ший	пра́вило
		плохо́й	пра́во
		междунаро́дный	му́зыка
			рабо́та

Разгово́р

3.5–5. Listen to the dialogue and fill in the missing words.

То́мас: Ма́ша, каки́е предме́ты ты ________________ в университе́те?

Ма́ша: В э́том семе́стре я изуча́ю ________________ , ________________,
________________ и ________________. А что ты изуча́ешь?

То́мас: ________________, коне́чно. А ещё ________________
и ________________.

Ма́ша: Очень интере́сно! Я то́же бу́ду ________________ э́ти предме́ты в янва́ре.

Урок 6

Verb люби́ть — to love

The verb **люби́ть** — *to love* is a 2nd conjugation verb (It conjugates like **говори́ть**.). Its **я-form** has an additional-**л**- letter and the stressed ending. Other present tense forms have stress on the stem. Past tense is regular with stable stress on the stem.

Present tense

Personal Pronouns	люб**и́ть**
я	любл-**ю́**
ты	лю́б-**ишь**
он, она́, кто	лю́б-**ит**
мы	лю́б-**им**
вы	лю́б-**ите**
они	лю́б-**ят**

Что ты лю́бишь?

Я люблю́ рок-му́зыку.

Кого́ ты лю́бишь?

Я люблю́ ма́му.

Past tense

Gender/Number	люб**и́ть**
m.	люби́-**л**
f.	люби́-**ла**
n.	люби́-**ло**
pl.	люби́-**ли**

Ра́ньше То́мас люби́л джаз.

Ра́ньше Ма́ша люби́ла поп-му́зыку.

А что вы люби́ли ра́ньше?

Люби́ть is used with

a direct object: **люби́ть кого́? что?** — *love whom? what?* (Ма́ша лю́бит ма́му.);

or a verb infinitive: **люби́ть де́лать что?** — *love to do what?* (Я люблю́ чита́ть.).

More examples:

Ра́ньше Ма́ша люби́ла поп-му́зыку, а тепе́рь она́ лю́бит рок-му́зыку.

Ди́ма лю́бит игра́ть. Ма́ша лю́бит слу́шать му́зыку. Юми лю́бит петь*. *to sing

Анна Алекса́ндровна и Ива́н Петро́вич лю́бят чита́ть газе́ты.

3.6–1. Кто что лю́бит? Complete the sentences using the correct form of люби́ть in the present tense.

1. Ма́ма ______________ чай и сыр.
2. Ди́ма ______________ молоко́ и шокола́д.
3. Ба́бушка и де́душка ______________ слу́шать но́вости.
4. Студе́нты ______________ отдыха́ть.
5. Что ты ______________ де́лать?
6. Вы ______________ рок-му́зыку?
7. Я ______________ изуча́ть ру́сский язы́к.
8. Мы ______________ говори́ть по-ру́сски.

Что вы лю́бите? Likes and dislikes

3.6–2. Что я люблю́ и не люблю́.

А. Sort the following foods and drinks in two groups: the ones that you like and those that you don't like. Remember to change the ending for the accusative case where necessary.

Молоко́, чай, сок, пи́во (beer), во́дка, шокола́д, сыр, хлеб, борщ, я́блоки, бана́ны, лимо́ны, апельси́ны, о́вощи, рис, ры́ба, колбаса́ (sausage).

Я люблю́ ____

____.

Я не люблю́ ____

____.

Б. Working with a dictionary find two more food items to add to your list of likes and two food items to add to your list of dislikes.

А ещё я люблю́ ______________________ и ______________________.

Я не люблю́ ______________________ и ______________________.

Поговори́м! Let's talk!

3.6–3. Что ты лю́бишь есть? Что ты лю́бишь пить? Discuss with a classmate what you like and don't like to eat or drink. Take turns asking and answering questions:

> Что ты лю́бишь **есть?** — *What do you like to eat?*
> Что ты лю́бишь **пить?** — *What do you like to drink?*
>
> **Есть** and **пить** are two irregular verbs. You will learn how to conjugate them later on. For now, you can use these verbs after любить in their infinitive forms.

Поговори́м! Let's talk!

3.6–4. Ты лю́бишь де́лать дома́шнюю рабо́ту? Discuss with a classmate what you like and don't like to do. Ask each other Yes/No questions to create a conversation similar to the one in the model. Use the verbs listed. Take turns asking and answering.

Образе́ц:

— Ты лю́бишь де́лать дома́шнюю рабо́ту?

— Нет, не люблю́. А ты лю́бишь слу́шать му́зыку?

— Да, люблю́. А ты лю́бишь... ?

> чита́ть
> рабо́тать
> отдыха́ть
> изуча́ть
> слуша́ть
> расска́зывать

Verb петь — to sing

The verb **петь** — *to sing* belongs to the 1st conjugation. Its present tense forms, however, have different root vowel (-**о**-) and stressed endings in all forms. Its past tense is regular with stable stem stress.

Present tense

Personal Pronouns	пе**ть**
я	по-ю́
ты	по-ёшь
он, она́, кто	по-ёт
мы	по-ём
вы	по-ёте
они	по-ю́т

When a 1st conjugation verb has **stressed ending**, its vowel-**е**- in all middle forms becomes -**ё**-: ты по**ёшь**, он по**ёт**, мы по**ём**, вы по**ёте**.

Что ты поёшь?

Я пою́ ру́сскую наро́дную* пе́сню*
**folk, *song*

Past tense

Gender/Number	пе**ть**
m.	пе-л
f.	пе́-ла
n.	пе́-ло
pl.	пе́-ли

Вчера́ мы пе́ли ру́сские наро́дные пе́сни.

Петь can be used with a direct object: **петь что?** — *sing what?*

Земфи́ра поёт но́вую пе́сню.

The verb is often accompanied by a descriptive adverb: **петь как?** — *sing how?*

Она́ о́чень хорошо́ поёт.

3.6–5. Кто как поёт? Complete sentences using the correct form of **петь** in the present tense.

1. Анна Алекса́ндровна __________ хорошо́.
2. Ива́н Петро́вич __________ пло́хо.
3. Де́ти __________ ве́село.
4. Юми __________ о́чень краси́во.
5. А как вы __________?
6. Мы __________ гро́мко*. *loudly
7. А как ты __________?
8. Я __________ __________.

3.6–6. Listen to the text and fill in the missing words.

Вчера́ у Ма́ши до́ма __________ вечери́нка*. Там __________ То́мас, Юми и други́е студе́нты — друзья́ Ма́ши. Они́ слу́шали му́зыку и __________ ру́сские наро́дные и совреме́нные пе́сни. То́мас гро́мко и ве́село __________ "Кали́нку"*, а Юми краси́во __________ пе́сню «По́люшко по́ле»*.

*party

*Kalinka

*Meadowland

Урок 7

Повторя́ем. Chapter 3 Review

This section summarizes what you should be able to understand and say after completing **Тéма 3**. For additional practice, vocabulary building and self-tests, please go to Спутник website.

1. Слу́шаем и понима́ем

Listen to the following conversations to hear Masha, Yumi, and Thomas talking about their personalities, musical and reading preferences.

Listening tips:

- Read and understand the questions first.
- Listen to the conversation for the first time, and figure out what is being discussed.
- With questions in mind, listen again for specific information.
- Write down your answers. (You don't have to answer in full sentences.)
- Listen one more time to check your answers.

А. Ма́ша расска́зывает како́й она́ челове́к и что она́ лю́бит. Listen to Masha's story and answer the questions about her.

1. Како́й Ма́ша челове́к? Что говоря́т друзья́ и что ду́мает Ма́ша?
2. Как Ма́ша отдыха́ет?
3. Каку́ю му́зыку она́ слу́шает?

Б. Юми расска́зывает како́й она́ челове́к и что она́ лю́бит. Listen to Yumi's story and answer the questions about her.

1. Како́й Юми челове́к?
2. Что Юми чита́ет?
3. Какую му́зыку она́ слу́шает?
4. Каку́ю пе́вицу лю́бит слу́шать Юми?

В. То́мас расска́зывает како́й он челове́к и что он лю́бит. Listen to Thomas's story and answer the questions about him.

1. Како́й То́мас челове́к?
2. Что он лю́бит де́лать?
3. Каку́ю му́зыку он слу́шает?
4. Кто его́ люби́мый гитари́ст?
5. Каки́е англи́йские и росси́йские гру́ппы он слу́шает?

2. Чита́ем вслух

In this section, you will find longer words broken down into their smaller syllables. Read them aloud to master their pronunciation. Phrases and intonation contours follow the syllable reading exercise. Exercises are complemented by recordings posted on the book's website.

Слу́шаем и чита́ем

А. Practice reading the following words and word combinations aloud. Listen to the recording, and imitate the pronunciations of the words.

у-пра-жне́-ни-е, пре-дло-же́-ни-е, пе-ре-во́д, пра́-ви-ло, но́-во-сти

ве-сё-лый, серь-ёз-ный, по-ле́з-ный, о-па́с-ный, тру́д-ный, ва́ж-ный

смеш-но́й, прос-то́й, пло-хо́й, боль-шо́й

ма́-лень-кий, рос-си́й-ский, до-ма́ш-ний

до-ма́ш-ня-я ра-бо́-та, клас-си́-чес-ка-я му́-зы-ка, сов-ре-ме́н-ный жур-на́л

ге́н-дер-ны-е ис-сле́-до-ва-ни-я, меж-ду-на-ро́д-ны-е от-но-ше́-ни-я

ис-кус-ство-ве́-де-ни-е, му-зы-ко-ве́-де-ни-е, пра-во-ве́-де-ни-е

Б. Practice reading the following phrases aloud. Remember to use the proper intonation.

1. Какой[2] вы челове́к?
2. Я серьёзный[1] челове́к.
3. Что[2] вы лю́бите?
4. Какую[2] му́зыку вы слу́шаете?
5. Вы хорошо[3] поёте?
6. Вы слу́шаете русскую[3] или французскую[1] му́зыку?

7. Я слу́шаю ру́сскую[3], япо́нскую[3], англи́йскую[3] и францу́зскую[1] му́зыку.
8. А испа́нскую[4]? — Да, коне́чно[1]. Я люблю́ испа́нскую гита́ру[1]. А вы[2]? Вы лю́бите[3] испа́нскую гита́ру?

3. Что мы изуча́ли

Before you read

1. Take one minute to scan through Part 1 (**Часть 1**) and tell the names of characters discussed in the text and make comments about their characters (in Russian).
2. Take one minute to scan through Part 2 (**Часть 2**) and tell what adjectives and verbs are being discussed there.

Часть 1

На́ша те́ма — «Како́й вы челове́к? Что вы лю́бите?». Мы чита́ли те́ксты, слу́шали диало́ги, де́лали упражне́ния.

Мы говори́ли о том, каки́е профе́ссии интере́сные, тру́дные, ва́жные, поле́зные, опа́сные. Мы расска́зывали о себе́: что мы лю́бим есть и пить, что чита́ем, каку́ю му́зыку слу́шаем.

Мы узна́ли*, что Ма́ша хоро́шая студе́нтка. Она́ чита́ет ру́сские и англи́йские журна́лы, слу́шает ру́сскую, англи́йскую, францу́зскую му́зыку. Ма́ша лю́бит рок, блюз и джаз. Её люби́мая певи́ца — Земфи́ра.

*learned, found out

Юми из Япо́нии — серьёзный челове́к. Она́ чита́ет газе́ты, журна́лы, но́вости в Интерне́те, и, коне́чно, кни́ги. Кста́ти*, она́ чита́ет по-япо́нски, по-англи́йски и по-ру́сски. Юми лю́бит популя́рную и класси́ческую му́зыку.

*by the way

То́мас из Кана́ды — весёлый челове́к. Он музыка́нт, игра́ет на гита́ре, лю́бит класси́ческий рок. Его люби́мый гитари́ст Джи́мми Пейдж игра́л в рок-гру́ппе «Led Zeppelin».

Часть 2

Мы изучáли нóвую граммáтику: мнóжественное* числó*, падéж*, рýсские прилагáтельные*. Падéж — э́то óчень трýдная тéма. Тéма «Прилагáтельные» не трýдная, но рýсские прилáгательные иногдá óчень длúнные*. Напримéр: талáнтливый, классúческий, совремéнный, мáленький.

*plural, *number *case
*adjectives
*long

А ещё мы изучáли нóвые глагóлы: любúть и петь. Любúть — óчень полéзный и вáжный глагóл. Прáвда*? Как вы дýмаете?

*Is this true?

After you finish reading

Answer the following questions in Russian:

1. Что читáет Мáша? Какýю мýзыку онá слýшает?
2. Какóй человéк Юми? Что онá читáет? Какýю мýзыку слýшает?
3. Какýю мýзыку лю́бит Тóмас? Кто егó любúмый гитарúст?
4. Падéж — э́то трýдная тéма?
5. Какúе прилагáтельные вы хорóшо знáете?
6. Какúе прилагáтельные вы плóхо знáете?
7. Какúе нóвые глагóлы вы изучáли?

4. Учим слова

Russian and English Cognates

Russian has many English cognates (or international words). Many words for school subjects and professions are English-Russian cognates. These words are easy to recognize and understand as they sound similar to each other in English and Russian. Learn to pronounce such cognates "the Russian way" when you speak Russian. Pay attention to where the stress is because it is often different from the stress in English.

Слушайте и повторяйте.

те́ма	актёр	профе́ссия
текст	актри́са	гру́ппа
диало́г	бизнесме́н	рок
студе́нт	инжене́р	блюз
грамма́тика	компози́тор	джаз
компью́тер	космона́вт	гита́ра
журна́л	президе́нт	гитари́ст
журнали́ст	профе́ссор	му́зыка
	спортсме́н	музыка́нт

These Russian words for professions are very similar to their English equivalents. However, they have different vowels stressed. For example, in English word **architecture** the emphasis (stress) is on the first '**a**' while in Russian **архитекту́ра** the emphasis in on '**у**'. Practice pronouncing these words properly in Russian. Focus on the word stress.

Слушайте и повторяйте.

архитекту́ра	медици́на	социоло́гия
журнали́стика	педаго́гика	филоло́гия
истори́я	политоло́гия	филосо́фия
литерату́ра	психоло́гия	хи́мия

Despite the fact that all adjective cognates have additional Russian "endings" added, they are still recognizable.

Слушайте и повторяйте.

ру́сский	интере́сный
англи́йский	серьёзный
класси́ческий	

Word Formation

Many Russian adjectives are derived from other words, mostly nouns and verbs. Learn to guess the meaning of a new word with a familiar root. For example: **любо́вь** — *love*, **люби́ть** — *to love*, **люби́мый** — *1) favourite, 2) beloved.*

Here is an exercise for you to practice making educated guesses. Give the English equivalents for Russian word combinations in the chart based on the meaning of nouns with the same root as adjectives.

Noun (Russian)	Noun (English)	Phrase (Russian) adjective + noun	Phrase (English) adjective + noun
му́зыка	*music*	музыка́льный теа́тр	
дом	*house, home*	дома́шняя рабо́та	
ум	*mind, intellect*	у́мный студе́нт	
тала́нт	*talent*	тала́нтливый музыка́нт	
смех	*laughter*	смешно́й расска́з	
труд	*labour, work*	тру́дный тест	

Building Vocabulary

Note the derivatives[1] , and group them together. Create a section in your notebook where you collect words that share the same root. You can start your collection with these words:

1. петь — *to sing*
   певе́ц/певи́ца — *singer*
   пе́сня — *song*

   Моя́ люби́мая певи́ца поёт но́вую пе́сню.

2. му́зыка — *music*
   музыка́нт — *musician*
   музыка́льный — *music, musical*

   Я люблю́ рок-му́зыку.
   Мой друг — музыка́нт.

1 Derivative is a word that is derived from another word.

Flashcards

Remember to make flashcards for new adjectives and verbs you learned in this chapter. For each word/phrase, include the stress marks, context, and translation/image/explanation on the reverse side.

Your adjective flashcards should look similar to this:

Front side	*Reverse side*
весёлый весёлый дядя́	*joyful, happy* 

It's a good idea to include present tense forms of verbs in your flashcard. You only need three: **я**, **ты** and **они́**. You can easily restore all middle forms if you know the **ты**-form. Here is an example of a verb flashcard:

Front side	*Reverse side*
петь (пою́, поёшь, пою́т) Она́ краси́во поёт.	 *to sing*

Чита́ем и понима́ем. Reading the lyrics "Я полюби́ла Вас" *I fell in love with you* by Земфи́ра

Read aloud the lyrics to the song **Я полюби́ла Вас** by the Russian poet and musician **Земфи́ра**. You will find the link to the song on this chapter webpage. Remember all the reading rules you have learned: reduction of unstressed vowels, consonant assimilation and final consonant devoicing. You will find many new words, unknown cases, even participles! Don't be discouraged by this, you can still read and understand the poem. Learn to predict the meaning of new words and structures by relying on what is known to you and also on the provided translation of the poem.

Я полюби́ла Вас

Ме́дленно, ве́рно газ
Плыл по уста́вшей ко́мнате
Не задева́я глаз,
Тех, что Вы вряд ли вспо́мните.

Би́лся неро́вно пульс,
Мы́сли каза́лись го́лыми.
Из пистоле́та грусть
Це́лилась пря́мо в го́лову.

Стро́чки лете́ли вниз,
Ма́том руга́лись дво́рники.
Я выбира́ла жизнь,
Сто́я на подоко́ннике.

В у́тренний со́нный час,
В час, когда́ всё расста́яло,
Я полюби́ла Вас,
Мари́на Цвета́ева.

I fell in love with you

Slowly, surely gas
Was floating through the tired room
Not touching the eyes,
The ones you would hardly remember.

Pulse was beating irregularly,
Thoughts seemed to be naked.
Out of the gun sadness
Was pointing straight into the head.

Lines were falling down,
Yardmen were swearing.
I was choosing life
Standing on the windowsill.

In the sleepy morning hour,
In the hour when everything melted away,
I fell in love with you,
Marina Tsvetaeva.

Земфи́ра Талга́товна Рамаза́нова
Совреме́нный поэ́т, музыка́нт, певи́ца.
Живёт и рабо́тает в Москве́.

Мари́на Ива́новна Цвета́ева
Поэ́т, проза́ик, перево́дчик XX ве́ка

Комме́нтарии

Capitalized Вы

In writing, the pronoun Вы and its forms (**Вас, Вам, Ва́ми**) are often capitalized to show respect to the addressee. In this poem the author (**Земфи́ра**) addresses the poet from the past whom she loves and respects. The capital Вы emphasizes that attitude. Вы is also capitalized in formal invitations, greeting cards, etc.

Words with familiar roots

Look for words with familiar roots. You should know these words:
у́тро — *morning*, у́тром — *in the morning*
жить — *to live*
по́мнить — *to remember*
окно́ — *window*
люби́ть — *to love*
вре́мя — *time*

In the poem, find the words derived from those listed above. Discuss with your teacher and classmates their meanings. How is each pair similar and different?

Зада́ние 1. In this poem, find and read aloud the examples of:

a) words with unstressed, and therefore reduced, vowels о, е, and я and

b) words with a devoiced final consonant.

Зада́ние 2. Find three adverbs and two adjectives used in this poem. How do you know that they are either an adjective or an adverb?

Тема 4

Где вы живёте, учитесь и работаете?

Практика

- **Где вы живёте?** Talking about where people live
- **Где вы у́читесь?** Talking about where people study
- **Факульте́ты. Ка́федры.** Faculties. Departments
- **Где вы рабо́таете?** Work places

Грамматика

- The verb **жить** — *to live*
- The verb **учи́ться** — *to study*. Verbs with **-ся**. Introduction
- **На како́м ку́рсе?** — What year of study?
- The prepositional case of nouns and adjectives
- The personal and possessive pronouns
- Study verbs: **учи́ться** vs. **изуча́ть** vs. **занима́ться**
- Future tense. Introduction

Культура

- Education in Russia. **Образова́ние в Росси́и**

Читаем и понимаем

- Reading Russian proverbs and folk tale **"Репка"**, *The Turnip*

Акти́вный слова́рь. Те́ма 4

Nouns
Места́ рабо́ты и учёбы — Places of Work and Study
Что?

акаде́мия — *academy*

аспиранту́ра — *graduate school, postgraduate studies*

банк — *bank*

библиоте́ка — *library*

больни́ца — *hospital*

институ́т — *institute*

заво́д — *plant, factory*

ка́федра — *department*

ко́лледж — *college*

комме́рческая фи́рма — *commercial firm, company*

компа́ния — *company*

консервато́рия — *conservatory*

косми́ческая ста́нция — *space station*

лаборато́рия — *laboratory*

магази́н — *store*

министе́рство — *ministry*

о́фис — *office*

поликли́ника — *policlinic*

рестора́н — *restaurant*

телеви́дение — *TV broadcast, television*

туристи́ческая фи́рма (турфи́рма) — *travel agency*

факульте́т — *faculty*

фе́рма — *farm*

фи́рма — *firm*

юриди́ческая фи́рма — *law firm*

Профе́ссии — Professions / Occupations
Кто?

библиоте́карь — *librarian*

гид-экскурсово́д — *tourist guide*

лабора́нт — *laboratory assistant*

ме́неджер — *manager*

рабо́чий — *1) worker; 2) working*

секрета́рь — *secretary*

фе́рмер — *farmer*

учени́к — *pupil*

учёный — *scientist*

фе́рмер — *farmer*

Other Nouns
Что?

го́род — *city, town*

зда́ние — *building*

иде́я — *idea*

кварти́ра — *apartment*

ко́мната — *room*

курс — *course*

образова́ние — *education*

общежи́тие — *dormitory*

о́пера — *opera*

план — *plan*

страна́ — *country*

Verbs
Что де́лать?

изуча́ть (изуча́ю, изуча́ешь, изуча́ют) — *to study a subject*

занима́ться (занима́юсь, занима́ешься, занима́ются) — *to study, do homework*

поговори́ть (поговорю́, поговори́шь, поговоря́т) — *to talk, have a chat*

учи́ться (учу́сь, у́чишься, у́чатся) — *to study, be a student*

Adjectives
Како́й факульте́т? Which Faculty?

гуманита́рный — *Humanities*

инжене́рный — *Engineering*

истори́ческий — *History*

лингвисти́ческий — *Linguistic*

математи́ческий — *Mathematics*

медици́нский — *Medical*

музыка́льный — *Music*

педагоги́ческий — *Education*

политологи́ческий — *Political Science*

психологи́ческий — *Psychology*

социологи́ческий — *Sociology*

физи́ческий — *Physics*

филологи́ческий — *Philology (languages and literatures)*

филосо́фский — *Philosophy*

экономи́ческий — *Economics*

юриди́ческий — *Law*

Како́й курс? What year of study?

пе́рвый — *first*

второ́й — *second*

тре́тий — *third*

четвёртый — *fourth*

пя́тый — *fifth*

шесто́й — *sixth*

Other Adjectives
Како́й?

иностра́нный — *foreign*

мла́дший — *younger*

ста́рший — *older*

туристи́ческий — *tourist (adj.)*

Possessive Pronouns
Чей? Чья? Чьё? Чьи?

мой (моя́, моё, мои́) — *my, mine*

твой (твоя́, твоё, твои́) — *your, yours*

наш — *our*

ваш — *your, yours*

его — *his*

её — *her*

их — *their*

чей (чья, чьё, чьи) — *whose*

Prepositions

в — *in, at*

на — *on, in, at*

о (об) — *about*

Урок 1

Ма́ша живёт в но́вой кварти́ре в Москве́.

Она́ рабо́тает в на́шем о́фисе.

То́мас живёт в но́вом до́ме в Ванку́вере.

Он у́чится в на́шем кла́ссе.

Где вы живёте? Talking about where people live

Я живу́ в Ло́ндоне. Мои́ роди́тели живу́т в Калифо́рнии.
Ма́ша живёт в Москве́.

To say what town / city you live in, change the name of the town as shown below.

Ло́ндон — в Ло́ндоне — add **е** after final consonant

Москв**á** — в Москв**é** — change final **а** to **е**

Калифо́рн**ия** — в Калифо́рн**ии** — change final **ия** to **ии**

Фра́нц**ия** — во Фра́нц**ии**

Где?		
Ø	→	е
а	→	е
ия	→	ии

в (**во**) — *in*
в becomes **во** before a consonant cluster if the first letter in the cluster is either **в** or **ф**: во **Вл**адивосто́ке, во **Фл**о́риде, во **Фр**а́нции

You will learn more about these endings later in this chapter (prepositional case). For now, follow the above model and ask your teacher to help when in doubt.

4.1–1. Где он живёт? Где она́ живёт? Say what cities these people live in. Follow the model given below in the Образе́ц.

Образе́ц: Ка́рлос, Мадри́д. Ка́рлос **живёт в** Мадри́д**е**.

1. Сюза́нна, Копенга́ген
2. Тиму́р, Анкара́
3. Хосе́, Бу́энос-Айрес
4. Джейн, Вашингто́н
5. Еле́на, Флоре́нция
6. Джон, Ме́льбурн
7. Мо́ника, Варша́ва
8. Мо́рган, Отта́ва
9. Ива́н, Влади́мир
10. Ке́йко, Оса́ка

Compound names spelled with a hyphen (like Буэнос-Айрес, Нью-Йорк) change their last part only: в Буэнос-Айрес**е**, в Нью-Йорк**е**.

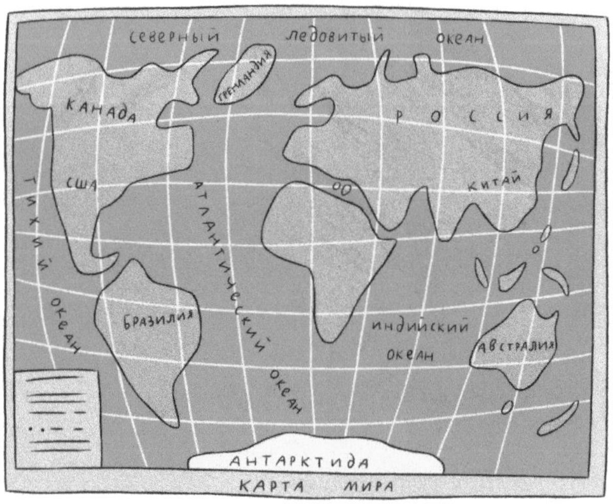

Поговори́м! Let's talk!

4.1–2. Вы хорошо́ зна́ете геогра́фию? In groups of 3-4 students, discuss where these cities are located. Choose the correct location (country) for each city. Take turns reading and answering questions.

- If you know the answer, say: **Я зна́ю, что...** — *I know that...*
- If you don't know, take a guess and say: **Я ду́маю, что...** — *I think that...*
- Correct your group mate if you think his / her guess is wrong.
- In 5 minutes, compare your group answers with other groups in class.

1. Где Копенга́ген?

а) в Испа́нии

б) в Да́нии

в) в Аргенти́не

2. Где Ме́льбурн?

а) в Австра́лии

б) в Испа́нии

в) в Ме́ксике

3. Где Анкара́?

а) в Ту́рции

б) в Аргенти́не

в) в Гре́ции

4. Где Варша́ва?

а) в По́льше

б) в Че́хии

в) в Болга́рии

5. Где Буэ́нос-Айрес?

а) в Ту́рции

б) в Аргенти́не

в) в Испа́нии

6. Где Отта́ва?

а) в США

б) в Кана́де

в) в Англии

7. Где Вашингто́н?

а) в Австра́лии

б) в Кана́де

в) в США

8. Где Но́вгород?

а) в Болга́рии

б) в Че́хии

в) в Росси́и

9. Где Флоре́нция?

а) в Росси́и

б) в Ита́лии

в) в Гре́ции

10. Где Оса́ка?

а) в Росси́и

б) в Кита́е

в) в Япо́нии

11. Где Со́чи?

а) в Че́хии

б) в По́льше

в) в Росси́и

12. Где Ливерпу́ль?

а) в Англии

б) в США

в) в Ита́лии

The Verb **жить** — *to live*

Жить — *to live* is a 1st conjugation verb with the end stress in the present tense. First conjugation verbs with final syllable stress have-**ё**- in **ты**, **он**, **мы** and **вы** forms (instead of-**е**-).

The present tense forms of **жить** have additional letter-**в**- added to stem. Its **я** and **они** forms have-**у**- in the ending (instead of-**ю**-).

жи**ть**	1st conjugation		
Present tense		Past tense	
я	жив-у́	он, кто	жи-**л**
ты	жив-ё**шь**	она́	жи-**ла́**
он, она, кто	жив-ё**т**	оно́	жи́-**ло**
мы	жив-ё**м**	они́	жи́-**ли**
вы	жив-ё**те**		
они́	жив-у́**т**		

Note the end stress in the feminine form.

4.1–3. Где вы живёте? Use the correct present tense forms of the verb *to live* to complete the sentences.

1. Где вы ________________ ?
2. Мы ________________ в Калифо́рнии в Лос-Анджелесе.
3. Где ________________ ба́бушка и де́душка?
4. Они́ ________________ в Ки́еве.
5. Са́ша ________________ в Монреа́ле.
6. Моя́ ма́ма ________________ в Москве́.
7. Мои́ друзья́ ________________ в Санкт-Петербу́рге.
8. Где ты ________________ ?
9. Я ________________ .

4.1–4. Где вы жи́ли ра́ньше и где живёте тепе́рь? Say where these people lived before and where they live now. Use the correct present and past tense forms of the verb *to live* to complete the sentences.

Образе́ц: Ра́ньше Джон **жил** в Вашингто́не, а тепе́рь он **живёт** в Нью-Йо́рке.

1. Ра́ньше Андре́й ________________ в Но́вгороде, а тепе́рь он ________________ в Москве́.
2. Ра́ньше Оля ________________ в Москве́, а тепе́рь она́ ________________ в Ки́еве.
3. Ра́ньше Кири́лл и Ири́на ________________ в Санкт-Петербу́рге, а тепе́рь они́ ________________ в Сие́тле.
4. — Где вы ________________ ра́ньше? Где вы ________________ тепе́рь?

   — Ра́ньше мы ________________ в Ванку́вере, а тепе́рь мы ________________ в Викто́рии.
5. Ра́ньше я ________________,
   а тепе́рь я ________________ .

Урок 2

Где вы у́читесь? Talking about where people study

Я учу́сь в университе́те на экономи́ческом факульте́те.
Ма́ша у́чится в университе́те на лингвисти́ческом факульте́те.
Ма́ша у́чится на второ́м ку́рсе.

на — *at, in, on*

To say where you study, change the name of the school as shown below.

университе́т — в университе́т**е**	add **e** after final consonant
шко́л**а** — в шко́л**е**	change final **a** to **e**
акаде́м**ия** — в акаде́м**ии**	change final **ия** to **ии**

Где?	Ø	→	е
	а	→	е
	ия	→	ии

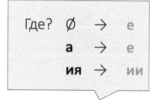

4.2–1. Где он у́чится? Где она́ у́чится? Say where these people study.

Образе́ц: Ма́ша, университе́т. Ма́ша **у́чится в** университе́т**е**.

1. То́мас, университе́т.
2. Ди́ма, шко́ла.
3. Джон, ко́лледж.
4. Андре́й, акаде́мия.
5. Мо́ника, институ́т.
6. Я учу́сь....

Факульте́ты. Ка́федры. Faculties. Departments

The name of a faculty (**факульте́т**) or a department (**ка́федра**) often becomes an adjective:

экономи́ческий факульте́т — *Business Faculty (or Faculty of Economics)*

английская ка́федра — *English Department*

Read the list of Russian equivalents of some popular faculties[1] and guess what they are in English.

гуманита́рный	политологи́ческий
инжене́рный	психологи́ческий
истори́ческий	социологи́ческий
компью́терный	физи́ческий
математи́ческий	филологи́ческий
медици́нский	филосо́фский
музыка́льный	экономи́ческий
педагоги́ческий	юриди́ческий

When a noun changes to answer the question **Где?** (to indicate location), the adjective must also change:

Я учу́сь на экономи́ческом факульте́те.
Я учу́сь на гуманита́рном факульте́те на англи́йской ка́федре.

Different universities have different faculty-department divisions. When using an adjective from the above list for department name, remember to change it into feminine: **истори́ческая ка́федра**.

For example, if you study in the Humanities Faculty in the department of History, you can refer to it as: **гуманита́рный факульте́т** and **истори́ческая ка́федра** in Russian.

Я учу́сь на гуманита́рном факульте́те на истори́ческой ка́федре.

---

1 Some names of faculties and departments cannot be turned into an adjective. For example, Faculty of Global Studies is translated as Факульте́т глоба́льных проце́ссов, or Faculty of International Relations as Факульте́т междунаро́дных отноше́ний. Consult your teacher for the best Russian equivalent of your faculty/department name.

4.2–2. На како́м факульте́те он(она́) у́чится? Say where these people study. Follow the model below.

Образе́ц: Иван, инжене́рный факульте́т.

Ива́н **у́чится на** инжене́рн**ом** факульте́т**е**.

1. То́мас, музыка́льный факульте́т.
2. Ма́ша, филологи́ческий факульте́т.
3. Джон, гуманита́рный факульте́т.
4. Андре́й, экономи́ческий факульте́т.
5. Мо́ника, медици́нский факульте́т.
6. Я учу́сь... *(your faculty name)*.

The Verb учи́ться — to study. Verbs with -ся. Introduction

Учи́ться (*to study*) is a 2nd conjugation verb with the reflexive particle-**ся** at the end. You will later learn the meanings of-**ся**. For the time being remember

- if a verb has-**ся** in the infinitive, it remains in all forms;
- -**ся** becomes-**сь** after a vowel.

The verb **учи́ться** has a shifted stress in the present tense: the stress falls on the ending in the **я**-form and shifts to the stem in other present tense forms. In the past tense, **учи́ться** has stable stem stress.

The **я**-form of the verb has-**у**- in the ending (instead of-**ю**-). The **они́** form has-**а**- in the ending (instead of-**я**-). Compare: я говор**ю́** but я уч**у́**сь, они говор**я́**т but они́ у́ч**а**тся.

учи́**ться**	2st conjugation		
Present tense		Past tense	
я	уч-**у́**-**сь**	он, кто	учи́-**л**-**ся**
ты	у́ч-**ишь**-**ся**	она́	учи́-**ла**-**сь**
он, она, кто	у́ч-**ит**-**ся**	оно́	учи́-**ло**-**сь**
мы	у́ч-**им**-**ся**	они́	учи́-**ли**-**сь**
вы	у́ч-**ите**-**сь**		
они	у́ч-**ат**-**ся**		

4.2–3. Где вы у́читесь? Use the correct present tense forms of the verb *to study* to complete the following sentences.

1. Где вы ____________________ ?
2. Мы ____________________ в университе́те.
3. Где ____________________ Джон?
4. Где ____________________ Са́ра?
5. Джон и Са́ра ____________________ на гуманита́рном факульте́те.
6. Где ____________________ твои́ друзья́? — Они́ ____________________ в ко́лледже.
7. Моя́ сестра́ ____________________ в шко́ле.
8. Где ты ____________________ ?
9. Я ____
____________________ . *(give as many details as you can)*

4.2–4. Где они́ учи́лись? Use the correct past tense forms of the verb *to study* to complete the sentences.

1. Моя́ тётя ____________________ в университе́те в Аризо́не.
2. Мой дя́дя ____________________ в ко́лледже в Калифо́рнии.
3. Где ____________________ твои́ роди́тели?
4. Они́ ____________________ в ко́лледже в Торо́нто.

Поговори́м! Let's talk!

4.2–5. Где вы учи́лись ра́ньше и где вы у́читесь тепе́рь? With a partner, discuss where you went to school before and where you go to school now? Mention the type of school (шко́ла, ко́лледж, университе́т) and the city. Take turns reading and answering questions. Your conversation should be similar to this:

— Я учи́лась в шко́ле в Ха́рькове, а тепе́рь я учу́сь в универси́тете в Ки́еве. А где ты учи́лся?

— Я учи́лся в шко́ле в Ми́нске, а тепе́рь учу́сь в университе́те в Ванку́вере.

На како́м ку́рсе? — What year of study?

— На како́м ку́рсе ты у́чишься? — *What year of study are you in?*

— Я учу́сь на пе́рвом ку́рсе. — *I'm in my first year.*

To talk about the year of study, you need to learn the ordinal numbers. Russian ordinal numbers look and function like adjectives. Memorize the ordinal numbers 1-6, and note their case forms (prepositional case).

	Како́й?	**На како́м ку́рсе?**
first	пе́рвый	на пе́рв**ом**
second	второ́й	на втор**о́м**
third	тре́тий	на тре́ть**ем**
forth	четвёртый	на четвёрт**ом**
fifth	пя́тый	на пя́т**ом**

Note:
- end stress in второ́й (**на второ́м**)
- soft ending in тре́тий (**на тре́тьем**)

The prepositional case is used in the answer for both the ordinal number and the word **курс**, which in this context means *"year"*, not *"course"*. The preposition **на** is used for *"in"*:

Я учу́сь **на** пе́рв**ом** ку́рс**е**.
Мой брат у́чится **на** четвёрт**ом** ку́рс**е**.

If you are a graduate student, you should use the word **аспиранту́ра** (graduate school).

Я учу́сь в аспиранту́ре. — *I'm in grad school.*

4.2–6. На ка́ком ку́рсе они́ у́чатся? Formulate grammatically correct sentences based on the information provided.

1. Иван и Серге́й — second year
2. Ната́ша и Та́ня — third year
3. Анто́н — forth year
4. Мари́на — first year
5. Я — ?

Поговори́м! Let's talk!

4.2–7. Ask 3-4 of your classmates what year of study they are in. Take turns asking and answering.

Жизнь в Росси́и: лю́ди, исто́рия, культу́ра
Образова́ние в Росси́и. Education in Russia

Шко́ла

Russian children are accepted to school (**шко́ла**) from age 6.5 and start in grade 1, and they attend the same school building for the entire eleven years. Education is placed high among Russians.

The first of September—annual back-to-school day—is celebrated as a national holiday **День зна́ний** (*Day of Knowledge*). All children arrive to school dressed up bringing flowers for their teachers. For grade 1 students and their families, it is a very special day. The day begins with a school opening ceremony accompanied by music and various performances.

Students who go to **шко́ла** are called **шко́льники** (not **студе́нты!**): **шко́льник** is a schoolboy and **шко́льница** is a schoolgirl. Schooling is free and all **шко́льники** receive textbooks on loan from their school.

The Russian word for a school teacher is **учи́тель / учи́тельница**. For the first four years of primary school, **нача́льная шко́ла** students have the same **учи́тель** (except for music, physical education, and sometimes foreign languages). Starting from grade 5, different subjects are taught by subject specialists.

All students must take a Single State Examination **Еди́ный госуда́рственный экза́мен**, (**ЕГЭ**) in order to graduate from **шко́ла** and get accepted into **университе́т** or **ко́лледж**. It is a country-wide test in the Russian language, Mathematics, and one other subject of the students' choice. Successful students with good grades for their **ЕГЭ** get accepted to a **вуз** (**вы́сшее учёбное заведе́ние** — *higher educational institution*) the Russian term for university or college type of institution.

Университе́т и други́е ву́зы

The Russian abbreviation **вуз** (**вы́сшее уче́бное заведе́ние** — *higher educational institution*) is used for an academic institution where students study for 4–6 years to earn a degree in their chosen field. Russian **ву́зы** include: **университе́т**, **акаде́мия**, **институ́т**. We use the term **университе́т** to talk about higher education in Russia but similar principles apply to Russian **акаде́мия** and **институ́т**.

University students (**студе́нты**) receive free education (They have to be **росси́йские гра́ждане**.). **Студе́нты** are paid a stipend (**стипе́ндия**) and receive rooms in dormitories. The amount they get paid depends on the university's budget and student's academic progress (Good students get more money, and a single C grade will eliminate a student's stipend for the next school year.). **Стипе́ндия** is relatively small, and students are often financially supported by their parents or find a part time job to support themselves. Some universities accept students with lower **ЕГЭ** grades, but these students must pay a significant tuition fee and receive no stipend.

Уче́бный план

Росси́йские ву́зы have very strict curriculum (**уче́бный план)**. Each student declares his or her area of specialization upon entrance, and the courses are preselected for them based on the declared specialization. Students may take some electives outside of their major fields, but the number of such courses is very limited. Switching from one field to another is difficult because credits in one subject may not be applicable to another (One would have to start a new program form the beginning taking all preselected courses in the new field.). This system is not very flexible but provides very good specialty training. Students who focus on their chosen fields for 4–6 years of study make good specialists.

Undergraduate research is encouraged: each year, beginning in the second year of study, students write a course paper **курсова́я рабо́та**. In the last year, as part of completion of a degree, each student writes a major research paper **дипло́мная рабо́та** to demonstrate his/her understanding of a field. These projects are taken seriously, and students are given the entire final semester to do research and write their diploma thesises.

Иностра́нные языки́ в ву́зах

A study of a foreign language **иностра́нный язы́к** is required in both **шко́ла** and **университе́т**. University students normally study a foreign language for 2–3 years for three hours a week as part of their degree regardless of the area of specialization. The most popular language is English, followed by German and French. Interest in Chinese and Japanese is growing. Students who chose a foreign language as their specialization normally have language classes for 14–18 hours per week.

Чита́йте те́кст. Кто где рабо́тает и у́чится.

Это ру́сская семья́. Вы уже́* немно́го зна́ете э́ту семью́. Ива́н Петро́вич — инжене́р. Он рабо́тает на заво́де*. Его́ жена́ — Анна Алекса́ндровна — врач. Она́ рабо́тает в поликли́нике*. Они́ живу́т в Москве́.

*already
*factory
*policlinic (outpatient)

Их ста́ршая* дочь Ма́ша — студе́нтка. Ма́ша у́чится в университе́те на фи-ло-ло-ги́-че-ском факульте́те. Их мла́дший* сын Ди́ма — шко́льник. Он у́чится в шко́ле в шесто́м кла́ссе.

*older
*younger

Вопросы

1. Где рабо́тает Ива́н Петро́вич?
2. Где рабо́тает его́ жена́?
3. Где у́чится их ста́ршая дочь?
4. На како́м факультете у́чится Ма́ша?
5. Где у́чится их мла́дший сын?
6. В како́м кла́ссе у́чится Ди́ма?

Слу́шайте и чита́йте диало́ги.

1. Где рабо́тают твой роди́тели?

Юми: Ма́ша, у тебя́ о́чень прия́тные роди́тели! Твоя́ ма́ма сказа́ла, что она́ врач. Она́ рабо́тает в больни́це*?

*hospital

Маша: Нет, ма́ма рабо́тает не в больни́це, а в поликли́нике. Она́ де́тский врач-терапе́вт*.

*pediatrician

Юми: Наве́рное, э́то тру́дная рабо́та.

Маша: Я то́же так ду́маю. Но ма́ма лю́бит э́ту рабо́ту.

Юми: А где твой па́па рабо́тает?

Маша: Па́па рабо́тает на заво́де. Он инжене́р.

2. Твои́ роди́тели то́же музыка́нты?

Маша: То́мас, а твои́ роди́тели то́же музыка́нты?

Томас: Да. Па́па компози́тор. Он рабо́тает в консервато́рии и до́ма. Ма́ма учи́тель му́зыки. Она́ рабо́тает в шко́ле. А ещё она́ о́чень хорошо́ поёт. В мо́лодости она́ пе́ла в о́пере, да́же сейча́с иногда́ поёт.

Маша: Очень интере́сно!

3. Вопро́сы к диало́гам.

1. Ма́ма Ма́ши рабо́тает в больни́це и́ли в поликли́нике?
2. Её па́па рабо́тает в шко́ле и́ли на заво́де?
3. Где рабо́тает па́па То́маса?
4. Где рабо́тает ма́ма То́маса? Что она́ хорошо́ де́лает?

Урок 3

The Prepositional Case of Nouns and Adjectives

- **Где? — *Where?***

To indicate location, the **prepositional case** is used. It answers the question **Где?** *Where?* Study the following sentences:

Ма́ша живёт в Москве́.	*Masha lives in Moscow.*
Subject — Location	Subject — Location
Я учу́сь в университе́те.	*I study at university.*
Subject — Location	Subject — Location
Ма́ма рабо́тает в шко́ле.	*Mom works at school.*
Subject — Location	Subject — Location

Note that location can be understood broadly: **в словаре́** (*in the dictionary*), **в Интерне́те** (*on the Internet*), **в сло́ве** (*in the word*). Study the additional examples with the prepositional case below:

Посмотри́ в словаре́.	*Look it up in the dictionary.*
Она́ чита́ет но́вости в Интерне́те.	*She reads the news on the Internet.*
В э́том сло́ве есть бу́ква Ж.	*There is the letter Ж in this word.*

- **О ком? — *About whom?* О чём? *About what?***

Prepositional case is also used for objects of the preposition **о** (*about*) and answers the questions **О ком?** (*about whom?*) and **О чём?** (*about what?*).

Это расска́з о соба́ке.	*This is a story about a dog.*
Мы говори́ли о му́зыке.	*We were talking about music.*

The preposition **о** becomes **об** before vowels **а**, **о**, **у**, **э**, **и**: **об** истории, **об** университете.

Мы говори́ли об университе́те.	*We were talking about university.*

Prepositional case must **always** occur with a preposition.

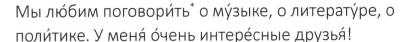

Чита́йте те́кст. Где мы живём и у́чимся. Расска́зывает ру́сская студе́нтка Ма́ша.

Read the text and identify all examples of prepositional case. Underline them.

Я живу́ в Москве́ в ста́рой кварти́ре и учу́сь в университе́те. Я учу́сь на филологи́ческом факульте́те, изуча́ю англи́йский язы́к и литерату́ру.

Мои́ друзья́ То́мас и Юми то́же у́чатся в университе́те. То́мас у́чится на музыка́льном факульте́те, а Юми на экономи́ческом. Они́ иностра́нные* студе́нты и живу́т в общежи́тии*.

*foreign
*dormitory

Мы лю́бим поговори́ть* о му́зыке, о литерату́ре, о поли́тике. У меня́ о́чень интере́сные друзья́!

*talk, have a chat

Вопро́сы

From the text above, write out two different noun endings and two different adjective endings for prepositional case.

Prepositional noun endings: ____ , ____ . Examples: ________________________________ .

Prepositional adjective endings: ____ , ____ . Examples: ____________________________ .

Поговори́м! Let's talk!

1. Где живёт Ма́ша?
2. Где у́чится Ма́ша?
3. На како́м факульте́те она́ у́чится?
4. На како́м факульте́те у́чится То́мас?
5. На како́м факульте́те у́чится Юми?
6. Где живу́т То́мас и Юми?
7. О чём Ма́ша, То́мас и Юми лю́бят поговори́ть?

Prepositional Case Endings of Nouns and Adjectives
Regular Forms

The following chart shows regular hard stem prepositional case forms of nouns and adjectives.

Gender / Number	Nominative	Prepositional
Masculine	но́в**ый** дом	в но́в**ом** до́м**е**
Neuter	но́в**ое** сло́в**о**	в но́в**ом** сло́в**е**
Feminine	но́в**ая** кварти́р**а**	в но́в**ой** кварти́р**е**
Plural	но́в**ые** дом**а́**, слов**а́**, кварти́р**ы**	в но́в**ых** дом**а́х**, слов**а́х**, кварти́р**ах**

Notes

- All case endings in Russian have hard and soft variants. Hard stem endings shown in the chart above are most common. Study the examples of **soft stem nouns** below. Singular soft endings are the same as hard (-**е** for all genders) but plural soft endings have -**ях** at the end:

Singular Soft (Nom. → Prep.)		**Plural Soft (Nom. → Prep.)**	
слова́р**ь**	→ в словар**е́**	словар**и́** — в словар**я́х**	
стать**я́**	→ в стать**е́**	стать**и́** — в стать**я́х**	
пла́ть**е***	→ в пла́ть**е**	пла́ть**я** — в пла́ть**ях**	**dress*

- Feminine nouns ending in-**ия** and neuter nouns ending in-**ие** in the nominative singular take the ending-**ии** in the prepositional case:

  Росс**и́я** → в Росс**и́и**
  упражне́н**ие** → в упражне́н**ии**

  When such nouns form plural, their prepositional plural ending is-**ях**: в упражне́ни**ях**.

- Foreign geographical names ending in-**о**,-**и**,-**у** are indeclinable:

  Торо́нт**о** – в Торо́нт**о**, Ка́лгар**и** – в Ка́лгар**и**, Бак**у́** – в Бак**у́**.

4.3–1. **A.** Choose -**е** or -**ии** for the prepositional singular ending of nouns below. Explain your choice.

Образе́ц: шко́ла — в шко́ле

> **страна́** — *country*
> **общежи́тие** — *dormitory*
> **зда́ние** — *building*

университе́т — в ...	страна́ — в ...
ко́лледж — в ...	исто́рия — в ...
акаде́мия — в ...	компа́ния — в ...
общежи́тие — в ...	зда́ние — в ...
семья́ — в ...	календа́рь — в ...

Б. Choose **-ах** or **-ях** for the prepositional plural ending of nouns listed above. Explain your choice.

Образе́ц: шко́ла — в шко́лах

4.3–2. Choose the correct prepositional case ending (**-ом**, **-ой**, or **-ых**) for the adjectives below.

Образе́ц: но́вый дом — в но́в**ом** до́ме

интере́сная статья́ — в ______________________ статье́

тру́дное упражне́ние — в ______________________ упражне́нии

смешно́й расска́з — в ______________________ расска́зе

ста́рые кварти́ры — в ______________________ кварти́рах

Spelling Rules and Exceptions

- **The 7-letter spelling rule**

  Remember 7-letter rule when you form prepositional plural of adjectives (we cannot write **-ы** after **к**, **г**, **х**, **ж**, **ш**, **ч**, **щ**, so we must write **-и** instead):

больш**и́е**	→	в больш**и́х**
хоро́ш**ие**	→	в хоро́ш**их**
ма́леньк**ие**	→	в ма́леньк**их**
плох**и́е**	→	в плох**и́х**

ки	жи
ги	ши
хи	чи
~~ы~~	щи

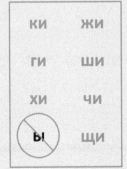

- **The 5-letter spelling rule**

  After the hushing consonants **ж**, **ш**, **ч**, **щ** and the consonant **ц**, write **е** in place of **о** if the ending is not stressed. You know one such adjective so far **хоро́ший** (*good*):

в хоро́шем до́ме в хоро́шей кварти́ре

ме́сто — *place*

в хоро́шем ме́сте

- **Adjectives with soft -н-**

  Adjectives in -**ний**, keep their endings soft in all forms. So far you have seen one such adjective m. дома́ш**ний**, f. дома́ш**няя**, n. дома́ш**нее**, pl. дома́ш**ние** (*home*):

  в дома́шнем перево́де в дома́шней рабо́те

  в дома́шнем упражне́нии в дома́шних рабо́тах

- Indeclinable nouns never change:

  в метро́, в такси́, в пальто́.

4.3–3. Choose the correct prepositional case ending (-**ом** / -**ем**, -**ой** / -**ей**, or -**ых** / -**их**) for the adjectives listed below. Remember the spelling rules and exceptions. Explain your choice of endings.

Образе́ц: но́вая шко́ла — в но́в**ой** шко́ле (feminine, hard stem)
больши́е кварти́ры — в больш**и́х** кварти́рах (plural, 7-letter rule)

интере́сное ме́сто — в ______________________ ме́сте

просто́е упражне́ние — в ______________________ упражне́нии

смешна́я исто́рия — в ______________________ исто́рии

дороги́е кварти́ры — в ______________________ кварти́рах

больши́е города́ — в ______________________ города́х

ста́рые дома́ — в ______________________ дома́х

хоро́ший университе́т — в ______________________ университе́те

ма́ленький слова́рь — в ______________________ словаре́

Дава́йте поигра́ем! Let's play a game!

4.3–4. Working with a partner, create the longest possible sentence describing the place you live in (дом, кварти́ра, общежи́тие, зда́ние, го́род, страна́). This place can be real or imagined. Your sentence must be logical and grammatically correct. To make the sentence longer, use as many descriptive words (adjectives) as you can.

Образе́ц: Я живу́ в **большо́м ста́ром краси́вом** до́ме.

You have 3 minutes to write down your sentence. When you have finished, read your sentence aloud. Other students in class should count how many adjectives you used in your description. The pair with the longest sentence wins the game.

Где вы рабо́таете? Work Places

Мой па́па врач. Он рабо́тает **в** больни́ц**е**.

Моя́ ма́ма учи́тельница. Она́ рабо́тает **в** шко́л**е**.

Мой дя́дя фе́рмер. Он рабо́тает **на** фе́рм**е**.

To say where you work, use the preposition **в** followed by workplace in the prepositional case. Note that some places require **на** instead of **в**.

4.3–5. Match the professions on the left with the workplaces on the right. Create meaningful sentences as in the model.

Образе́ц: Врач рабо́тает в больни́це.

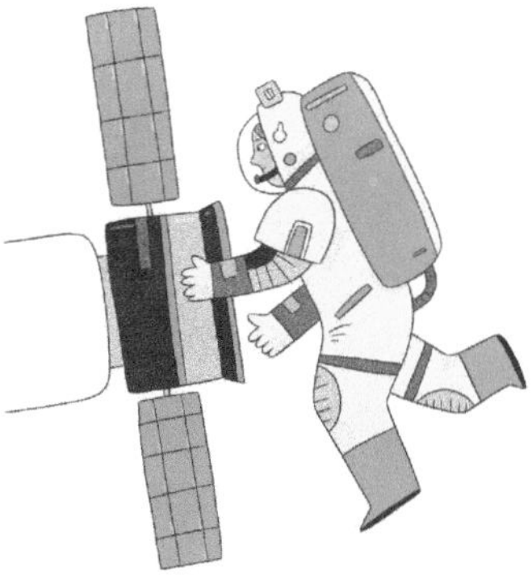

актёр	в ба́нке
актри́са	в библиоте́ке
библиоте́карь	в больни́це
бизнесме́н	в газе́те
гид-экскурсово́д	в комме́рческой фи́рме
врач	в лаборато́рии
журнали́ст	в магази́не
инжене́р	в министе́рстве
компози́тор	в о́фисе
космона́вт	в теа́тре
лабора́нт	в туристи́ческой фи́рме (турфи́рме)
ме́неджер	в университе́те
мини́стр	на косми́ческой ста́нции
музыка́нт	в юриди́ческой фи́рме
певе́ц	

певи́ца	на заво́де
писа́тель	в шко́ле
перево́дчик	на ра́дио
преподава́тель	на телеви́дении
программи́ст	на фе́рме
продаве́ц	
профе́ссор	до́ма
секретáрь	
учи́тель	
фе́рмер	
юри́ст	

Поговори́м! Let's talk!

4.3–6. Working with a partner, find out what his/her relatives do for a living and where they work.

Образе́ц: — Кто по профе́ссии твоя́ ма́ма?
— Моя́ ма́ма ме́неджер.
— Где она́ рабо́тает?
— Она́ рабо́тает в магази́не.

Урок 4

The Personal and Possessive Pronouns

я

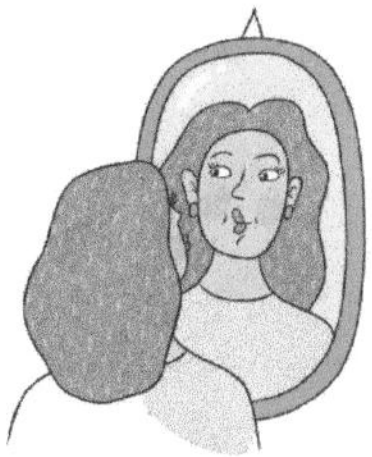

моя́ маши́на

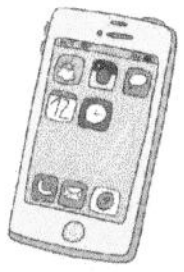

моё пла́тье

мой телефо́н

мои́ ту́фли

You have already seen most of the Russian personal and possessive pronouns. Review them with this chart.

Personal		Possessive	
Кто?	***Who?***	**Чей? Чья? Чьё? Чьи?**	***Whose?***
я	*I*	мой, моя́, моё, мои́	*my, mine*
ты	*you (sing.)*	твой, твоя́, твоё, твои́	*your, yours (sing. informal)*
он	*he, it (m.)*	его́	*his, its (m.)*
оно́	*it (n.)*	его́	*its (n.)*
она́	*she, it (f.)*	её	*her, its (f.)*
мы	*we*	наш, на́ша, на́ше, на́ши	*our, ours*
вы	*you (pl.)*	ваш, ва́ша, ва́ше, ва́ши	*your, yours (pl., sing. formal)*
они́	*they*	их	*their, theirs*

Notes and Reminders on Personal Pronouns

- The personal pronoun **вы** is used for both the plural and the singular formal / polite way of addressing a person. **Ты** is used to address one person informally.

  Вы говори́те по-ру́сски? *Do you speak Russian?* → *asking one person formally or asking more than one person*

  Ты говори́шь по-ру́сски? *Do you speak Russian?* → *asking one person informally*

- Russian has three pronouns for 'it': **он**, **она́**, **оно́**. The choice depends on the gender (masculine, feminine, or neuter) of the noun being replaced by pronoun.

Это наш но́вый учёбник. **Он** неплохо́й.	*This is our new textbook.* ***It****'s not a bad one.*
Это моя́ дома́шняя рабо́та. **Она́** не о́чень тру́дная.	*This is my homework.* ***It****'s not hard.*
Это но́вое общежи́тие. **Оно́** о́чень большо́е.	*This is our new dorm.* ***It****'s very big.*

Personal Pronouns in the Accusative and Prepositional Cases

Personal pronouns replace nouns, and like nouns, they change for cases. You've already seen the **accusative** case forms for most of the personal pronouns. These statements should be familiar to you:

Accusative phrase	Nominative form	Accusative form
Меня́ зову́т Ма́ша.	я	меня́
Как **тебя́** зову́т?	ты	тебя́
Как **его́** зову́т?	он, оно́	его́
Как **её** зову́т?	она́	её
Как **нас** зову́т?	мы	нас
Как **вас** зову́т?	вы	вас
Как **их** зову́т?	они́	их

More examples of personal pronouns in the accusative case:

Я люблю́ **тебя**. Я зна́ю **его**. Я понима́ю **вас**.

The following statements show how personal pronouns change for the **prepositional** case:

Prepositional phrase	**Nominative form**	**Prepositional form**
Он ду́мает обо **мне**.	я	во/обо **мне**
Он ду́мает о **тебе́**.	ты	в/о **тебе́**
Он ду́мает о **нём**.	он, оно́	в/о **нём**
Он ду́мает о **ней**.	она́	в/о **ней**
Он ду́мает о **нас**.	мы	в/о **нас**
Он ду́мает о **вас**.	вы	в/о **вас**
Он ду́мает о **них**.	они́	в/о **них**

More examples of personal pronouns in the prepositional case:

Это моя́ подру́га. Я говорю́ о **ней**.

Это Моско́вский университе́т. В **нём** у́чатся ру́сские и иностра́нные студе́нты.

4.4–1. Personal pronouns in the accusative case. Complete each sentence with the correct form of personal pronoun.

1. Ната́ша лю́бит ________________ . (он)
2. Ива́н хорошо́ зна́ет ________________ . (ты)
3. Мы пло́хо зна́ем ________________ . (она́)
4. Студе́нты лю́бят ________________ . (вы)
5. То́мас хорошо́ понима́ет ________________ . (мы)
6. Я по́мню ________________ . (они́)
7. Он пло́хо по́мнит ________________ . (я)
8. Ты по́мнишь ________________ ? (она́)

4.4–2. Personal pronouns in the prepositional case. Complete each sentence with the correct form of personal pronoun. Add prepositions where necessary.

1. Ната́ша ча́сто ду́мает ________________ . (он)
2. Ива́н ре́дко говори́т ________________ . (ты)
3. Мы не говори́м ________________ . (она)
4. Студе́нты мно́го говоря́т ________________ . (вы)
5. Твоя́ подру́га расска́зывала ________________ . (они́)
6. Твои́ друзья́ говори́ли ________________ . (мы)
7. Она́ не ду́мает ________________ . (я)
8. Что вы ду́маете ________________ ? (он)

Notes

ча́сто — *often*
ре́дко — *rarely*
мно́го — *a lot*
иногда́ — *sometimes*

Notes

говори́ть — *to talk (about something)*
расска́зывать — *to tell (a story about something/someone)*

4.4–3. Nominative, accusative or prepositional? Complete each sentence with the correct form of personal pronoun. Add prepositions where necessary.

всё равно́ — *anyways, no matter what*

1. Ма́ша лю́бит ________________ . (*you, sing.*)
2. Анто́н лю́бит ________________ . (*her*)
3. Роди́тели иногда́ не понима́ют ________________ (*me*), но я всё равно́ люблю́ ________________ . (*them*)
4. ____________ (*He*) ча́сто ду́мает ________________ (*about her*).
5. Студе́нты ча́сто говоря́т ________________ (*about you, formal*).
6. ____________ (*They*) не ду́мают ________________ (*about me*).
7. ________________ (*She*) не лю́бит ________________ (*me*).
8. Э́то но́вое общежи́тие. Я ________________ (*in it*) живу́.
9. ____________ (*We*) говори́ли ________________ (*about you, sing. informal*).
10. Извини́те, ______ (*I*) не по́мню ________________ (*you, formal*).

11. Это хоро́ший университе́т. ________________ (*In it*) учи́лись мои́ роди́тели.
12. Это хоро́шая шко́ла. ________________ (*In it*) у́чится мой брат.
13. Это тру́дное предложе́ние, но ________________ (*we*) хорошо́ понима́ем ________________ (*it*).
14. Это но́вое пра́вило. Я пло́хо понима́ю ________________ (*it*).
15. ________________ (*They*) о́чень талантли́вые музыка́нты. Мой друг расска́зывал ________________ (*about them*).

Notes and Reminders on Possessive Pronouns

- Russian does not make a distinction between *my/mine, your/yours, our/ours, or their/theirs.*
- The possessive pronouns **мой** (*my/mine*), **твой** (*your/yours sing. informal*), **наш** (*our/ours*), **ваш** (*your/yours pl., sing. formal*) and the question word **Чей?** (*whose?*) function like adjectives: they change form to agree in gender, number, and case with the nouns to which they refer. Dictionaries always list them in the masculine form.

  Это **мой** учéбник. Это **моя́** рабо́та. Это **моё** письмо́. Это **мои́** докумéнты.

  Чей э́то телефо́н? — **Мой**. *Whose phone is that? — Mine.*

  Чья э́то маши́на? — **Моя**. *Whose car is that? — Mine.*

- The possessive pronouns **его́** (*his*), **её** (*her/hers*), **их** (*their/theirs*) never change their form. The choice of a third person pronoun depends on the physical gender/number of people:

Это **его́** маши́на.

Это **её** маши́на.

Это **их** маши́на.

4.4–4. Supply the correct forms of **Чей.**

Образец: — **_Чья_** это кни́га?

1. ________________ э́то ту́фли?
2. ________________ э́то муж?
3. ________________ э́то ко́шка?
4. ________________ э́то роди́тели?
5. ________________ э́то письмо́?
6. ________________ э́то телефо́н?
7. ________________ э́то слова́рь?
8. ________________ э́то де́ти?

4.4–5. Supply the correct forms of **твой** (*your*) for the questions and **мой** (*my*) for the answers.

1. Это ________________ кни́га? — Да, ________________.
2. Это ________________ телефо́н? — Да, ________________.
3. Это ________________ пальто́? — Да, ________________.
4. Это ________________ тетра́ди? — Нет, не ________________.
5. Это ________________ соба́ка? — Да, ________________.
6. Это ________________ уче́бник? — Нет, не ________________.
7. Это ________________ ча́шка? — Да, ________________.
8. Это ________________ журна́лы? — Нет, не ________________.

4.4–6. Supply the correct forms of **ваш** (*your, plural*) for the questions and **наш** (*our*) for the answers.

1. Это ________________ дом? — Да, ________________.
2. Это ________________ маши́на? — Да, ________________.
3. Это ________________ общежи́тие? — Да, ________________.
4. Это ________________ кварти́ра? — Да, ________________.
5. Это ________________ кни́ги? — Нет, не ________________.
6. Это ________________ де́ти? — Нет, не ________________.
7. Это ________________ ко́шка? — Да, ________________.
8. Это ________________ ве́щи*? — Нет, не ________________. **things*

4.4–7. Translate into Russian. Remember that **его́**, **её**, and **их** do not change.

1. It's his brother. ______________________________
2. It's her mistake. ______________________________
3. It's their dog. ______________________________
4. It's my sister. ______________________________
5. It's your uncle. ______________________________
6. It's our car. ______________________________
7. It's your (*plural, formal*) dormitory.

   ____

8. Is that your (*informal*) sister?

   ____

4.4–8. Complete these mini-dialogues with the correct forms of the possessive pronouns.

1. — ____________ (*Whose*) э́то су́мка?

   — Это ____________ (*my*) су́мка.

2. — Извини́те, э́то ____________ (*your, formal*) телефо́н?

   — Да, ____________ (*mine*). Спаси́бо.

3. — Это ____________ (*my*) роди́тели.

   — Интере́сно. А как ____________ (*their*) зову́т?

4. — Ди́ма, где ____________ (*your, informal*) рюкза́к?

   — Не зна́ю. Наве́рное, я забы́л* ____________ (*it*) в шко́ле. **forgot, left*

5. — Вот ____________ (*your, informal*) молоко́.

   — Спаси́бо! А где ____________ (*my*) ча́шка?

   — Вот она́.

6. — Вот ____________ (*our*) дом. А здесь ____________ (*your, formal*) комна́та.

   — Спаси́бо. Здесь о́чень краси́во. А где ____________ (*your, formal*) де́ти?

Урок 5

Study Verbs: учи́ться vs. изуча́ть vs. занима́ться

There are three verbs in Russian that can be translated as *"to study"* into English: **учи́ться**, **изуча́ть**, **занима́ться**. These verbs are not interchangeable. Read the text below paying attention to the use of the *study* verbs.

Чита́йте текст. Где я учу́сь, что я изуча́ю. Расска́зывает япо́нская студе́нтка Юми.

Read the text and answer the questions (вопро́сы).

Меня́ зову́т Юми. Я студе́нтка из Япо́нии. Сейча́с я живу́ в Москве́ и **учу́сь** в Моско́вском университе́те на экономи́ческом факульте́те.

Я **изуча́ю** экономи́ку, ру́сский язы́к, литерату́ру и культу́ру.

Учи́ться в университе́те тру́дно, поэ́тому* я мно́го **занима́юсь**.

*that is why

Обы́чно* я **занима́юсь** в библиоте́ке два часа́ ка́ждый день: де́лаю дома́шнюю рабо́ту, чита́ю кни́ги, учу́ но́вые ру́сские слова́ и фра́зы.

*usually

Вопро́сы

1. Где у́чится Юми? В како́м университе́те?
2. На како́м факульте́те она́ у́чится?
3. Что она́ изуча́ет?
4. Учи́ться в университе́те тру́дно и́ли нет?
5. Юми мно́го занима́ется и́ли нет?
6. Где она́ обы́чно занима́ется?

Поговорим! Let's talk!

Using the questions below as guidelines, talk to a classmate about school. Take turns asking and answering the questions.

1. Где вы у́читесь? На како́м факульте́те вы у́читесь?
2. Что вы изуча́ете?
3. Как вы ду́маете, учи́ться в университе́те тру́дно и́ли нет?
4. Вы мно́го занима́етесь?
5. Где вы обы́чно занима́етесь: до́ма и́ли в библиоте́ке?

Now, fill in the chart below with the correct Russian *study* verb: **изуча́ть**, **учи́ться** or **занима́ться**?

Meaning	Russian *study* verb	Common context
be a student, go to school		в университе́те, в шко́ле
take a course in ..., study a subject		ру́сский язы́к, культу́ру, исто́рию, эконо́мику
prepare for classes, do homework		до́ма, в библиоте́ке мно́го

Notes

- To say how you are doing (well or poorly) at school, use **учи́ться**:

  Я хорошо́ учу́сь. — *I'm doing well at school (I'm a good student).*

- To say how hard you study, use **занима́ться**. Do not use **тру́дно** for *hard* but use **мно́го** (*a lot*) instead:

  Я мно́го занима́юсь. — *I study hard (I study a lot).*

  The adverb **тру́дно** can be used with **учи́ться**. The combination **тру́дно учи́ться** means *"it is hard/difficult to study"* but not *"I study hard"*. Compare:

  В университе́те тру́дно учи́ться. — *It is hard to study at university.*

  Я мно́го занима́юсь. — *I study hard (a lot).*

- The verb **занима́ться** is a 1st conjugation verb with the reflexive particle -**ся**. You know that -**ся** remains in all forms of the verb.

занима́**ться**	1st conjugation		
Present tense		**Past tense**	
я	занима́-ю-**сь**	он, кто	занима́-**л**-**ся**
ты	занима́-е**шь**-**ся**	она́	занима́-**ла**-**сь**
он, она, кто	занима́-е**т**-**ся**	оно́	занима́-**ло**-**сь**
мы	занима́-е**м**-**ся**	они́	занима́-**ли**-**сь**
вы	занима́-е**те**-**сь**		
они	занима́-ю**т**-**ся**		

4.5–1. The Russian language has many proverbs and sayings about learning. The verb **учи́ться** is often used to refer to the process of learning, acquiring knowledge. Read the Russian proverbs below, and try to match them with their English equivalents on the right.

1. Учи́ться никогда́ не по́здно.

2. Век живи́ — век учи́сь.

3. На оши́бках у́чатся.

A. *Live a century and learn a century.*

B. *We learn from our own mistakes.*

C. *It is never too late to learn.*

по́здно — *late*
letter [**д**] is silent

4.5–2. Как по-ру́сски? Translate the dialogue into Russian. You don't need to know the Russian words for 'go' and 'take' for this!

— Do you work or go to school?
— I go to university.
— What do you take?
— I take linguistics, history, and Russian.
— Do you study hard?
— Yes, I study 3 hours every day in the library or at home.
— You are a very good student!

Possessive Pronouns in the Accusative and Prepositional Cases

You already know that only feminine phrases (nouns and their modifiers) change for the accusative case. The following sample sentences show the modifier *my* used in the **accusative** case.

Профе́ссор чита́ет **мой** ру́сск**ий** перево́д.

Профе́ссор чита́ет **мою́** дома́шн**юю** рабо́т**у**.

Профе́ссор чита́ет **моё** пи́сьменн**ое** упражне́ние.

Профе́ссор чита́ет **мои́** прост**ы́е** те́ксты.

пи́сьменный — *written*

To form the accusative case of possessive pronouns, remember the simple rule that you learned for adjective and noun endings:

-я → -ю	мо**я́** → мою́, тво**я́** → твою́, чь**я** → чью	рабо́ту
-а → -у	на́ш**а** → на́шу, ва́ш**а** → ва́шу	рабо́ту
other → no change	мой, твой, наш, ваш, чей	перево́д
(Acc. = Nom.[2])	моё, твоё, на́ше, ва́ше, чьё	упражне́ние
	мои́, твои́, на́ши, ва́ши, чьи	те́ксты

4.5–3. Complete the sentences with the correct **accusative** case forms of the possessive pronouns.

1. Преподава́тель чита́ет ______________ (*your, informal*) рабо́ту.
2. Она́ слу́шает ______________ (*our*) диало́г.

2 This is true only if the noun being modified is **inanimate (i.e., not alive)**. Accusative endings of animate (i.e., alive) masculine and plural nouns with their modifiers coincide with genitive case endings. You will learn them later on.

3. Вчера́ ве́чером ба́бушка чита́ла ________________ (*my*) письмо́.
4. ________________ (*Whose*) статью́ вы чита́ли?
5. Мы чита́ли ________________ (*your, formal/plural*) кни́гу.
6. Студе́нты слу́шали ________________ (*your, informal*) расска́з.

The following chart introduces the **prepositional** case forms of the possessive pronouns **мой**, **твой**, **наш**, **ваш** and the question word **чей**.

Gender Number	Nominative case forms	Prepositional case forms	Endings
m.	чей (мой, твой, наш, ваш) дом	в чьём (моём, твоём, на́шем, ва́шем) до́ме	**-ём/-ем**
n.	чьё (моё, твоё, на́ше, ва́ше) письмо́	в чьём (моём, твоём, на́шем, ва́шем) письме́	
f.	чья (моя́, твоя, на́ша, ва́ша) кварти́ра	в чьей (мое́й, твое́й, на́шей, ва́шей) кварти́ре	**-ей**
pl.	чьи (мои́, твои́, на́ши, ва́ши) те́сты	в чьих (мои́х, твои́х, на́ших, ва́ших) те́стах	**-их**

4.5–4. Complete the sentences with the correct **prepositional** case forms of the possessive pronouns. Remember to add the prepositions (**в** or **о**).

1. Мой брат расска́зывал ________________ (*about your, formal*) семье́.
2. ________________ (*In whose*) тестах есть ошибки?
3. Кто живёт ________________ (*in your, informal*) до́ме?
4. Где слова́рь? — Он ________________ (*in my*) рюкзаке́.
5. ________________ (*In our*) кварти́ре о́чень больши́е о́кна.
6. ________________ (*In your, formal*) перево́де есть оши́бки.

4.5–5. Complete the sentences with the correct forms (accusative or prepositional) of the possessive pronouns.

1. Мы чита́ли ______________ (*your, formal*) статью́.
2. Мы говори́ли о ______________ (*your, formal*) статье́.
3. Они́ говори́ли о ______________ (*our*) рабо́те.
4. Преподава́тель чита́л ______________ (*her*) перево́д.
5. Де́душка чита́л ______________ (*my*) письмо́.
6. Она́ хорошо́ по́мнила ______________ (*our*) встре́чу*. **meeting*
7. В ______________ (*their*) до́ме живу́т иностра́нные студе́нты.
8. ______________ (*Whose*) рабо́ту вы чита́ете?
9. Мы не зна́ли о ______________ (*his*) пробле́мах.
10. В ______________ (*whose*) рабо́те была́ э́та оши́бка?
11. Моя́ сестра́ у́чится в ______________ (*your, informal*) кла́ссе.
12. Он рабо́тает в ______________ (*our*) общежи́тии.

Урок 6

Future Tense. Introduction

- Что ты **бу́дешь де́лать** за́втра?
- За́втра я **бу́ду рабо́тать**.

The future tense is used to describe an action that will take place in the future. Russian verbs have two future tenses: imperfective and perfective. **Imperfective future** refers to actions that do not emphasize the result while **perfective future** emphasizes the speaker's intention to complete an action in the future. From this lesson, you will learn how to use and form imperfective future tense. You will learn about perfective future later on.

Imperfective future tense

Imperfective future is used for actions in the future that do not emphasize the result. Russian imperfective future tense corresponds to three English future aspects:

In Russian	In English
Я бу́ду рабо́тать.	*I will work.* *I will be working.* *I will have been working.*

Study the following English future sentences and their Russian translations.

- Simple future: — Imperfective future:

  *She **will study** Russian in Moscow.* — Она́ **бу́дет изуча́ть** ру́сский язы́к в Москве́.

- Future progressive: — Imperfective future:

  *Tomorrow I **will be working**.* — За́втра я **бу́ду рабо́тать**.

- Future perfect progressive: — Imperfective future:

  *By summer, I **will have been working** here for two years.* — К ле́ту я **бу́ду рабо́тать** здесь **уже́** два го́да.

уже́ — *already* is used to express the meaning similar to "***will have being working***"

Russian imperfective future is formed with the verb **to be** followed by a verb **infinitive**. Study the imperfective future forms of the verb **рабо́тать** (*to work*).

рабо́тать	
Imperfective future tense	
я	бу́д-у рабо́тать
ты	бу́д-**ешь** рабо́тать
он, она́, кто	бу́д-**ет** рабо́тать
мы	бу́д-**ем** рабо́тать
вы	бу́д-**ете** рабо́тать
они	бу́д-**ут** рабо́тать

To list several things that you are planning on doing, say **бу́ду** once and list all verb infinitives after it:

За́втра я **бу́ду** <u>чита́ть</u>, <u>смотре́ть</u> телеви́зор и <u>отды́хать</u>.	*Tomorrow I **will** <u>read</u>, <u>watch</u> TV, and <u>relax</u>.*

4.6–1. Complete the sentences with the future verb phrase in parenthesis.

1. Что вы ______________________ (*will be doing*) за́втра ве́чером?
2. Ма́ша ______________________________ (*will be studying*) до́ма.
3. То́мас и Юми ________________________ (*will be reading*) по-ру́сски.
4. Ди́ма __________________________________ (*will be watching*) телеви́зор и ______________________ (*playing*).
5. Я ____.

Разговóр

4.6–2. А. Маша and Томас are discussing plans for tomorrow. Listen to their conversation, and fill in the blanks with the missing words.

Мáша: — Привéт, Тóмас! Как жизнь?

Тóмас: — Привéт, Мáша! Всё в порядке, спасибо. А как ты?

Мáша: — У меня всё отлично. Какие у тебя плáны на зáвтра*? *for tomorrow

Тóмас: — Утром я в университéте, днём ________________ в библиотéке.

Мáша: — А вéчером?

Тóмас: — Вéчером я ________________ .

Мáша: — Что бýдешь дéлать?

Тóмас: — Навéрное, ________________ . А ты?

Мáша: — Ты знáешь, мы с Юми ________________ один стáрый рýсский фильм. Если хочешь*, приходи*. *if you want *come over

Тóмас: — Спасибо. Отличная идéя! А во скóлько?

Мáша: — В ________________ вéчера. Нормáльно?

Тóмас: — Да, конéчно. Большóе спасибо.

Мáша: — Отлично. Тогдá* до зáвтра. *then

Тóмас: — До зáвтра.

Б. Now, listen to this conversation again, and answer the questions in full sentences in Russian.

1. Где бýдет Тóмас зáвтра ýтром?
2. Что он бýдет дéлать днём?
3. Где Тóмас бýдет вéчером и что он бýдет дéлать?
4. Что бýдут дéлать Мáша и Юми?
5. What does **мы с Юми** mean? You have not learned this structure yet; try guessing.

Поговорим! Let's talk!

4.6–3. Что вы бýдете дéлать зáвтра?

А. Here is the list of verbs you have learned so far: говори́ть, дéлать, дýмать, занимáться, знать, изучáть, играть, отдыхáть, петь, пóмнить, понимáть, рабóтать, расскáзывать, слýшать, смотрéть, учи́ться, читáть.

From this list, choose five verbs that can be used to describe your day. Write them out.

1. ______________________________
2. ______________________________
3. ______________________________
4. ______________________________
5. ______________________________

Б. What will you be doing tomorrow in the morning, in the afternoon, in the evening? Make at least three statements about yourself. Write them down.

1. ____
2. ____
3. ____

В. Working with a partner, take turns asking and answering the following questions:

1. Что ты бýдешь дéлать зáвтра ýтром?
2. Что ты бýдешь дéлать зáвтра днём?
3. Что ты бýдешь дéлать зáвтра вéчером?

Урок 7

Повторя́ем. Chapter 4 Review

This section summarizes what you should be able to understand and say after completing **Тема 4**. For additional practice, vocabulary building and self-tests, please go to Спутник website.

1. Слу́шаем и понима́ем

Listen to the conversations to hear Masha and Thomas talking about their studies and work.

Listening tips:

- Read and understand the questions first.
- Listen to the conversation for the first time, and figure out what is being discussed.
- With questions in mind, listen again for specific information.
- Write down your answers. (You don't have to answer in full sentences)
- Listen one more time to check your answers.

А. Ма́ша расска́зывает о рабо́те и учёбе. Listen to Masha's story and answer the questions below.

1. Где Ма́ша у́чится?
2. Где она́ подраба́тывает*? **works part time*
3. Кака́я профе́ссия Ма́ши?
   а) учи́тель
   б) гид-экскурсово́д
   г) перево́дчик
   д) библиоте́карь
4. Что Ма́ша говори́т о свое́й рабо́те?
   а) э́то не тру́дная рабо́та
   б) рабо́та помога́ет* изуча́ть англи́йский язы́к **helps*
   в) э́то о́чень интере́сная рабо́та

В. То́мас расска́зывает о жи́зни студе́нта в Кана́де. Listen to Thomas's story and answer the questions below.

1. Студе́нты в Кана́де пла́тят за образова́ние?
2. Где подраба́тывают студе́нты?
3. То́мас ду́мает, что интере́сно быть студе́нтом:
   а) в Росси́и
   б) в Кана́де
   в) в любо́й* стране́
4. Где рабо́тает То́мас? Что он де́лает?
5. Когда́ То́мас занима́ется?
   а) у́тром
   б) днём
   в) ве́чером, иногда́ но́чью

*any

плати́ть за образова́ние — *pay for education*

2. Чита́ем вслух

In this section, you will find longer words broken into syllables. Read them aloud to master their pronunciation. Phrases and intonation contours follow the syllable reading exercise. The exercises are complemented by recordings posted on the book's website.

Слушаем и читаем

A. Practice reading the following words and word combinations aloud. Listen to the recording, and imitate the pronunciations.

би-бли-о-те́-карь, экс-кур-со-во́д, пе-ре-во́д-чик, пре-по-да-ва́-тель, про-да-ве́ц

о-бра-зо-ва́-ни-е, у-ни-вер-си-те́т, фа-куль-те́т

гу-ма-ни-та́р-ный, ма-те-ма-ти́-че-ский, ме-ди-ци́н-ский, пе-до-го-ги́-че-ский

по-ли-то-ло-ги́-че-ский, пси-хо-ло-ги́-че-ский, со-ци-о-ло-ги́-че-ский, ю-ри-ди́-че-ский

он за-ни-ма́-е-тся, о-ни у́-ча-тся и ра-бо́-та-ют, он под-ра-ба́-ты-ва-ет

Б. Practice reading phrases aloud. Remember to use the proper intonation.

1. Где[2] вы живёте?
2. Вы у́читесь[3] и́ли рабо́таете[1]?
3. Где[2] вы у́читесь?
4. А ваш брат[4]?
5. Студе́нты подраба́тывают в кафе́[3], рестора́нах[3] и магази́нах[1].

3. Что мы изуча́ли

Before you read.

1. Take <u>two minutes</u> to scan through **Часть 1** and say whose parents are discussed in the text and where these parents work (in Russian).

2. Take <u>two minutes</u> to scan through **Часть 2** and say what long words are being discussed there.

Часть 1

На́ша те́ма — «Где вы живёте, у́читесь и рабо́таете?». Мы чита́ли те́ксты, слу́шали диало́ги, де́лали упражне́ния.

Мы говори́ли о том, где мы живём, у́чимся, рабо́таем, где живу́т, у́чатся и рабо́тают на́ши роди́тели и друзья́. Мы расска́зывали о себе́: на како́м факульте́те мы у́чимся, что изуча́ем, как мно́го занима́емся.

Мы узна́ли, что Ма́ша у́чится на филологи́ческом факульте́те и подраба́тывает ле́том в турфи́рме. Она́ перево́дчик и рабо́та помога́ет ей* акти́вно изуча́ть англи́йский язы́к. Па́па Ма́ши рабо́тает на заво́де, а ма́ма в поликли́нике. Её мла́дший брат Ди́ма у́чится в шко́ле в шесто́м кла́ссе.

*her, to her

А ещё мы узна́ли, где рабо́тают роди́тели То́маса. Его́ па́па — компози́тор. Он рабо́тает в консервато́рии и до́ма. Ма́ма То́маса — учи́тель му́зыки. Она́ рабо́тает в шко́ле.

Мы та́кже чита́ли и говори́ли об образова́нии в Росси́и. Интере́сно, что в Росси́и — одна́* шко́ла, где шко́льники у́чатся оди́ннадцать лет, а не три, как в Евро́пе и в Се́верной Аме́рике. Удиви́тельно*, что росси́йские студе́нты у́чатся в университе́те беспла́тно*. Это здо́рово*!

*one (f. of оди́н)
*it's surprising, amaz
*free, *cool, great

Часть 2

Мы изуча́ли но́вую грамма́тику: предло́жный* паде́ж, местоиме́ния*, бу́дущее* вре́мя*. Предло́жный паде́ж и бу́дущее вре́мя не о́чень тру́дные те́мы.

*prepositional, *pronouns, *future, *tense, time

Мно́гие* ру́сские слова́ похо́жи* на англи́йские. Наприме́р: факульте́т, университе́т, математи́ческий, физи́ческий, экономи́ческий, политологи́ческий. Эти слова́ не тру́дно понима́ть, но о́чень тру́дно чита́ть. Они́ таки́е* дли́нные!

*many, *look like

*so, *long

А ещё мы узна́ли, что в ру́сском языке́ три глаго́ла "study": учи́ться, изуча́ть и занима́ться. Ну́жно* говори́ть: «Я учу́сь в университе́те», «Я изуча́ю ру́сский язы́к», «Я мно́го занима́юсь». Это тру́дно запо́мнить*. Пра́вда? Как вы ду́маете?

*you have to

*memorize

After you finish reading

Answer the following questions in Russian:

1. О чём мы говори́ли, когда́ изуча́ли Те́му 4?
2. Что вы расска́зывали о себе́?
3. На како́м факульте́те у́чится Ма́ша? Где она́ подраба́тывает ле́том?
4. Где рабо́тают роди́тели Ма́ши?
5. Что вы узна́ли о роди́телях То́маса?
6. Ско́лько лет росси́йские шко́льники у́чатся в одно́й шко́ле?
7. Росси́йские студе́нты пла́тят за образова́ние?
8. Каки́е ру́сские слова́ похо́жи на англи́йские?
9. Каки́е три глаго́ла "study" вы зна́ете?

4. Учим слова

Word formation

Adjectival suffixes

A. Many nouns related to "area of studies" form adjectives with the suffix -**ическ**- and the appropriate adjective ending: биолог**и́ческ**ий, геолог**и́ческ**ий.

Form adjectives from nouns below. Remove the highlighted part of the noun and replace it with **-ический**.

геогра́ф**ия** — ______________

исто́р**ия** — ______________

матема́т**ика** — ______________

педаго́г**ика** — ______________

психоло́г**ия** — ______________

социоло́г**ия** — ______________

политоло́г**ия** — ______________

фи́з**ика** — ______________

филоло́г**ия** — ______________

эконо́м**ика** — ______________

Б. Other adjective suffixes include: **-н-**, **-льн-** and **-ск-**. Form adjectives from nouns by simply adding the appropriate suffix. If there is a highlighted part, remove it, and add the suffix.

-ный

инжене́р — ______________

компью́тер — ______________

-льный

шко́**ла** — ______________

му́зыка — ______________

-ский

медици́н**а** — ______________

филосо́ф**ия** — ______________

университе́т — ______________

В. Combine the adjectives on the left with the nouns on the right to create meaningful word combinations. Remember to change the adjective ending if necessary to agree with the noun. Some nouns can be combined with more than one adjective.

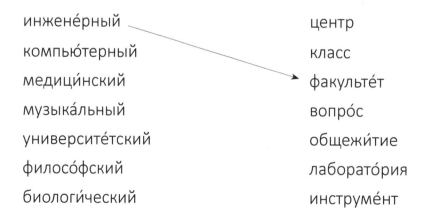

инжене́рный	центр
компью́терный	класс
медици́нский	факульте́т
музыка́льный	вопро́с
университе́тский	общежи́тие
филосо́фский	лаборато́рия
биологи́ческий	инструме́нт

Building Vocabulary

Add new words to your collection of derivatives:

1. учи́ться — *to study, be a university/college student*

   учёба — *studies, learning*

   учёный — *scientist, scholar*

   учи́тель — *teacher*

   учени́к — *pupil*

   Учи́тель и учени́к говоря́т об учёбе.

2. рабо́тать — *to work*

   рабо́та — *work, job*

   рабо́чий — *worker*

   Рабо́чие рабо́тают на заво́де.

3. занима́ться — *to study, prepare for classes, do homework*

   заня́тие (pl. заня́тия) — *1) class, classes; 2) occupation*

   за́нят, занята́, за́нято, за́няты — *to be busy*

   Ма́ша о́чень занята́. Она́ мно́го занима́ется.

Flashcards

It is easier to remember a new long word if you know what parts the word is made of. When making a flashcard for longer words, mark meaningful parts of the word (for example, you can use special symbols or colousrs to mark the word's root, suffix and ending). Your flashcard would look similar to this:

Front side	*Reverse side*
филосо́ф-ский Я учу́сь на филосо́фском факульте́те.	*philosophical*

Color pens, or markers would work as well for marking different parts of a word: философский. When reading a new long word, remember to break it into syllables: **фи-ло-со́ф-ский**.

Чита́ем и понима́ем. Reading Russian proverbs and folk tale "Ре́пка", *The Turnip*

Read the following Russian proverbs about work and learning. Compare them with the English translation provided. You will find them recorded on this chapter webpage. Remember the reading rules you have learned: reduction of unstressed vowels, consonant assimilation and final consonant devoicing.

Ру́сские посло́вицы	*Russian proverbs*
Рабо́та	***Work***
• Пти́цу узнаю́т в полёте, а челове́ка в рабо́те.	• *A bird is known by its flight, the man by his work.*
• Пчёлка ма́ленькая, а и та рабо́тает.	• *Although the bee is little, it is hard working.*
• Не ошиба́ется тот, кто ничего́ не де́лает.	• *He who does nothing makes no mistakes.*
Учёба	***Learning***
• На оши́бках у́чатся.	• *We learn from our mistakes.*
• Учи́ться никогда́ не по́здно.	• *It is never late to learn.*
• Век живи́ — век учи́сь.	• *Live a century, learn a century.*
• Учи́лся чита́ть да писа́ть, а вы́учился петь да пляса́ть.	• *He was learning to read and write but has learned to sing and dance.*
• Без букв и грамма́тики не у́чатся и матема́тике.	• *Without letters and grammar you can't learn even math.*
• Не сты́дно не знать, сты́дно не учи́ться.	• *It is not shame not to know, it is shame not to learn.*

Комментáрии

Russian proverbs

Originated from oral history and dating many centuries back, Russian proverbs and sayings reflect various aspects of national character and culture. Most proverbs were documented and studied in the 19th and 20th centuries. Russian lexicographer **Владúмир Ивáнович Даль** was the first to document the greatest number of proverbs and sayings. His two volume collection "**Послóвицы рýсского нарóда**" published in 1879 featured more than 30,000 entries.

Use of они forms of verbs for impersonal meaning

Russian proverbs avoid using personal pronouns. The **онú** form of the verb without the pronoun is commonly used to indicate impersonal meaning of the statement. It is especially common in proverbs and sayings. In English, such meaning is often conveyed by the passive voice structure.

Compare:

Птúцу узнаю́т в полёте, а человéка в рабóте.

A bird is known by its flight, the man by his work.

Other verb forms (such as imperatives, infinitives, **он** and **мы** forms without the pronoun) are also quite common in proverbs and sayings.

The word 'да' used for 'and'

You already know that '**да**' is commonly used for *and* in folk tales. It is also very common in proverbs and sayings:

Учúлся читáть да писáть, а вы́учился петь да плясáть.

He was learning to read and write but has learned to sing and dance.

Задáние 1. А. In the proverbs listed above, find the verbs related to the following nouns:

рабóта
учёба
ошúбка
письмó
пéсня

Б. What does each noun and verb mean?

Задáние 2. Can you think of the English equivalents for some of these proverbs? Discuss them with your classmates.

Read the popular Russian folk tale **"Ре́пка"** out loud. Remember the pronunciation rules you have learned: reduction of unstressed vowels, consonant assimilation and final consonant devoicing. You will find a recording of this tale on the webpage of this chapter.

Ре́пка
Ру́сская наро́дная ска́зка

The Turnip
A Russian folk tale

Посади́л дед ре́пку. Посади́л и говори́т: «Расти́-расти́ ре́пка сладка́, расти́-расти́ ре́пка крепка́».

Grandpa planted a turnip. He planted it and said: "Grow, grow my turnip: grow sweet, grow strong."

Вы́росла ре́пка сладка́, крепка́, больша́я-пребольша́я. Пошёл дед ре́пку рвать: тя́нет-потя́нет, вы́тянуть не мо́жет.

The turnip grew sweet, strong, and very-very big. Grandpa went to pull the turnip up: he pulls and pulls but cannot pull it up.

Позвáл дед бáбку. Бáбка за дéдку, дéдка за рéпку: тя́нут-потя́нут, вы́тянуть не мóгут.

Grandpa calls grandma. Grandma pulls grandpa, grandpa pulls the turnip. They pull and pull but cannot pull it up.

Позвалá бáбка внýчку. Внýчка за бáбку, бáбка за дéдку, дéдка за рéпку: тя́нут-потя́нут, вы́тянуть не мóгут.

Grandma calls the granddaughter. The granddaughter pulls grandma, grandma pulls grandpa, and grandpa pulls the turnip. They pull and pull but cannot pull it up.

Позвалá внýчка Жýчку. Жýчка за внýчку, внýчка за бáбку, бáбка за дéдку, дéдка за рéпку: тя́нут-потя́нут, вы́тянуть не мóгут.

The granddaughter calls the dog Zhuchka. Zhuchka pulls the granddaughter, the granddaughter pulls grandma, grandma pulls grandpa, and grandpa pulls the turnip. They pull and pull but cannot pull it up.

Позвалá Жýчка кóшку. Кóшка за Жýчку, Жýчка за внýчку, внýчка за бáбку, бáбка за дéдку, дéдка за рéпку: тя́нут-потя́нут, вы́тянуть не мóгут.

Zhuchka calls the cat. The cat pulls the dog, the dog pulls the granddaughter, the granddaughter pulls grandma, grandma pulls grandpa, and grandpa pulls the turnip. They pull and pull but cannot pull it up.

Позвалá кóшка мы́шку. Мы́шка за кóшку, кóшка за Жýчку, Жýчка за внýчку, внýчка за бáбку, бáбка за дéдку, дéдка за рéпку: тя́нут-потя́нут – и вы́тянули рéпку!

The cat calls the mouse. The mouse pulls the cat, the cat pulls the dog, the dog pulls the granddaughter, the granddaughter pulls grandma, grandma pulls grandpa, and grandpa pulls the turnip. They pull and pull, and they pull the turnip right up!

Комментáрии

Short-form adjectives

In this tale you have seen two examples of short-form adjectives: **сладкá** (*sweet*) and **крепкá** (*strong*). Their full forms are **слáдкий** and **крéпкий**. The short forms are used here after the notion of "to be".

> слáдкая рéпка – *sweet turnip*
>
> рaсти́ сладкá – *grow sweet*

You will learn more about various uses of short-form adjectives later.

Repetition

You already know about repetition as a peculiar feature of a folk tale. This tale is famous for its multiple repetitions of words and structures.

> расти́-расти́ ре́пка
>
> больша́я-пребольша́я
>
> тя́нут-потя́нут

Repetition in this tale is reinforced with the rhyming of the names of the participants: де́дка, ба́бка, вну́чка, Жу́чка, ко́шка, мы́шка.

The suffix пре-

The suffix **пре-** can be added to adjectives to intensify their meaning. Typically, an adjective with **пре-** follows the same word without the prefix with the hyphen between the two words.

> большо́й-пребольшо́й – *very-very big*
>
> сла́дкий-пресла́дкий – *very-very sweet*
>
> дли́нный-предли́нный – *very-very long*

Diminutives

As all Russian folk tales, this story uses many diminutive forms of nouns. Study the following examples.

Ре́пка (*dear turnip*) – derived form **ре́па** (*turnip*) and formed with the suffix-**к**-. You have seen diminutives of this type in the tale **"Ку́рочка Ря́ба"** where they refer to very small objects: **мы́шка** (*little mouse*) and **хво́стик** (*tiny/little tale*). In this story the turnip is giant (in English, the tale is often called "The Giant Turnip" or "The Enormous Turnip"). The diminutive here is used to reflect not the size of the turnip but the feeling of endearment and fascination.

Де́дка (*grandpa*) and **ба́бка** (*grandma*) are two diminutives derived from **дед** and **ба́ба**. In contemporary Russian, both forms have a pejorative connotation and are not recommended for addressing one's grandparents – **де́душка** and **ба́бушка** are used as affectionate words instead.

The words **вну́чка** (*granddaughter*) and **ко́шка** (*female cat*), as well as the popular dog's name **Жу́чка** are not formally diminutives but, in the sequence of repeated rhyming diminutives, one feels as if they are.

Русско-английский словарь

А

а — *but, and*
а́вгуст — *August*
Австра́лия — *Australia*
авто́бус — *bus*
акаде́мия — *academy*
актёр — *actor*
акти́вно — *actively*
акти́вный — *active*
актри́са — *actress*
Аля́ска — *Alaska*
Аме́рика — *America*
америка́нский — *American*
англи́йский — *English*
Англия — *England*
антрополо́гия — *anthropology*
апельси́н — *orange*
апре́ль — *April*
ара́бский — *Arabic*
Аргенти́на — *Argentina*
археоло́гия — *archeology*
архитекту́ра — *architecture*
аспира́нт — *graduate student (male)*
аспира́нтка — *graduate student (female)*
аспиранту́ра — *graduate school, postgraduate studies*
а́том — *atom*
аудито́рия — *lecture room, class room*

Б

ба́ба — *granny, peasant woman*
ба́бушка — *grandmother, grandma, granny*
балери́на — *ballerina*
бале́т — *ballet*
бана́н — *banana*
банк — *bank*
бар — *bar*
бежа́ть — *to run*
без — *without*
беспла́тно — *free of charge*
библиоте́ка — *library*
библиоте́карь — *librarian*
библиоте́чный — *library (adjective)*
бизнесме́н — *businessman*
биоло́гия — *biology*
бить — *to beat, hit*
би́ться — *to beat*
бли́зко — *close, nearby*
блюз — *blues*
Болга́рия — *Bulgaria*
больни́ца — *hospital*
большо́й — *big, large*
борщ — *borsch*
брат — *brother*
брать — *to take*
бу́дущий — *future*
бу́ква — *letter (character)*
бума́га — *paper*
буфе́т — *buffet, cafeteria*
бы́стро — *fast, quickly*
бы́стрый — *fast, quick*
быть — *to be*

В

в —in, at
ва́жно — *it's important*
ва́жный — *important*
ва́за — *vase*
ва́нна — *bathtub*
ваш — *your, yours*

Вашингто́н — *Washington*
век — *century*
велосипе́д — *bicycle*
ве́рно — *surely*
ве́село — *cheerfully*
весёлый — *cheerful, happy*
весе́нний — *spring (adjective)*
весна́ — *spring*
весь — *all, entire*
ве́чер — *evening, night*
вечери́нка — *get-together party*
ве́чером — *in the evening*
вещь — *thing*
ви́лка — *fork*
взро́слый — *adult*
вниз — *down*
Во ско́лько? — *At what time?*
вода́ — *water*
во́дка — *vodka*
вокза́л — *railway station, terminal*
вопро́с — *question*
восемна́дцать — *eighteen*
во́семь — *eight*
во́семьдесят — *eighty*
воскресе́нье — *Sunday*
воскреси́ть — *to resurrect*
воскре́сный — *Sunday (adjective)*
восто́к — *east*
вот — *here, here it is*
врач — *doctor*
вре́мя — *time*
вре́мя го́да — *season*
вряд ли — *unlikely*
все — *all*
всё — *everything, all*
Всё в поря́дке! — *Everything is all right!*
всё равно́ — *whatever, all the same*
вспо́мнить — *to recall, recollect, remember*
встре́титься — *to meet*
вто́рник — *Tuesday*
второ́й — *second*
вход — *entrance*
вчера́ — *yesterday*
вы — *you (plural, formal)*
выбира́ть — *to choose*
вы́мыт — *washed*
вы́учить — *to learn, have learned*
вы́учиться — *to have completed learning*
выходно́й — *day off*

Г

газе́та — *newspaper*
гвоздь — *nail*
где — *where*
ге́ндерные иссле́дования — *gender studies*
геогра́фия — *geography*
геоло́гия — *geology*
Герма́ния — *Germany*
гид-экскурсово́д — *tourist guide*
гимна́ст — *gymnast (male)*
гимна́стка — *gymnast (female)*
гита́ра — *guitar*
гитари́ст — *guitar player*
глаго́л — *verb*
глаго́л движе́ния — *verb of motion*
глаз (pl. глаза́) — *eye*
говори́ть — *to speak*
год — *year*
голова́ — *head*
го́лый — *naked*
го́род — *city, town*
гость — *guest*
граждани́н — *citizen*
грамма́тика — *grammar*
Гре́ция — *Greece*

гро́мко — *loudly*
гру́ппа — *group*
грусть — *sorrow, sadness*
гуманита́рный — *Humanities*

Д

да — *yes*
да (и) — *and*
давно́ — *long ago*
да́же — *even*
далеко́ — *far*
Да́ния — *Denmark*
дать — *to give*
да́ча — *summer cottage*
два — *two*
два́дцать — *twenty*
двена́дцать — *twelve*
дво́рник — *yardman*
девяно́сто — *ninety*
девятна́дцать — *nineteen*
де́вять — *nine*
дед — *grandfather*
де́душка — *grandfather, grandpa*
дека́брь — *December*
де́лать — *to do, make*
День рожде́ния — *Birthday*
де́сять — *ten*
де́ти — *children*
де́тский — *children (adjective), children's*
дешёвый — *cheap*
джаз — *jazz*
диало́г — *dialogue*
дли́нный — *long*
днём — *in the afternoon, in the daytime*
до — *until*
До встре́чи! — *See you! Until we meet!*
До за́втра! — *See you tomorrow!*
До свида́ния! — *Goodbye!*
До́брое у́тро! — *Good morning!*
до́брый — *kind, good*
До́брый ве́чер! — *Good morning!*
До́брый день! — *Good afternoon!*
дождь — *rain*
дом — *house*
до́ма — *at home*
дома́шний — *home (adjective)*
домо́й — *to home (answers куда́? — where to?)*
доро́га — *road, way*
дорого́й — *dear, expensive*
до́чка — *daughter (diminutive)*
дочь — *daughter*
драмату́рг — *playwright*
друг (pl. друзья́) — *friend*
друго́й — *another, other, different*
дру́жба — *friendship*
ду́ма — *thought*
ду́мать — *to think*
дя́дя — *uncle*

Е

Евро́па — *Europe*
его́ — *his*
еда́ — *food*
её — *her*
е́сли — *if*
есть — *1) to eat; 2) there is*
е́хать — *to go by a vehicle, drive*
ещё — *more; else*

Ё

ёлка — *fir-tree*

Ж

жар — *heat*
жена́ — *wife*

же́нский — *feminine, female*
живо́т — *stomach*
живо́тное — *animal*
жизнь — *life*
жи́ли-бы́ли — *once upon a time; lived and were*
жить — *to live*
журна́л — *journal; magazine*
журнали́ст — *journalist*
журнали́стика — *journalism*
журнали́стка — *journalist (female)*

З

за — *for*
заво́д — *plant, factory*
за́втра — *tomorrow*
задева́ть — *to touch*
занима́ться — *to study, do homework*
заня́тие — *1) class; 2) occupation*
за́пад — *west*
запо́мнить — *to remember, keep in mind*
защи́та — *defense, protection*
звать — *to call*
звук — *sound*
зда́ние — *building*
здесь — *here*
здо́рово — *awesome, cool*
Здра́вствуйте! — *Hello!*
зима́ — *winter*
зи́мний — *winter (adjective)*
зимова́ть — *to live through winter*
знако́миться — *to meet*
знать — *to know*
зна́чить — *to mean*
золото́й — *golden*
зуб — *tooth*

И

и — *and*
игра́ть — *to play*
игра́ть на — *to play an instrument*
иде́я — *idea*
идти́ — *to go, walk*
из — *from*
Извини́те — *Excuse me*
изуча́ть — *to study a subject*
и́ли — *or*
инжене́р — *engineer*
инжене́рный — *engineer (adjective)*
иногда́ — *sometimes*
иностра́нный — *foreign*
институ́т — *institute*
интере́сно — *it is interesting*
интере́сный — *interesting*
Интерне́т — *Internet*
информа́тика — *computer science*
искусствове́дение — *art studies*
Испа́ния — *Spain*
испа́нский — *Spanish*
иссле́дование — *research*
истори́ческий — *history (adjective), historical*
исто́рия — *history*
Ита́лия — *Italy*
италья́нский — *Italian*
их — *their*
ию́ль — *July*
ию́нь — *June*
каза́ться — *to seem, appear*
как — *how*

Й

йо́гурт — *yogurt*

К

как — *how*
Как дела́? — *How are you?*
Как жизнь? — *How is life?*
како́й — *what kind*
календа́рь — *calendar*
Кана́да — *Canada*
кана́дский — *Canadian*
каранда́ш — *pencil*
карто́фель — *potatoes*
кафе́ — *cafe*
ка́федра — *department*
кварти́ра — *apartment*
кенгуру́ — *kangaroo*
кино́ — *movie; movies*
Кита́й — *China*
кита́йский — *Chinese*
кларне́т — *clarinet*
класс — *class, group*
класси́ческий — *classical*
кла́ссно — *cool, awesome*
клуб — *club*
кни́га — *book*
когда́ — *when*
колбаса́ — *sausage*
ко́лледж — *college*
кома́нда — *1) team; 2) command*
кома́р — *mosquito*
коммента́рий — *comment*
комме́рческая фи́рма — *commercial firm, company*
ко́мната — *room*
компа́ния — *company*
компози́тор — *composer*
компью́терная те́хника — *computer equipment*
компью́терный — *computer (adjective)*
коне́чно — *of course*
консервато́рия — *conservatory*
конце́рт — *concert*
коро́ль — *king*
косми́ческая ста́нция — *space station*
космона́вт — *astronaut, cosmonaut*
ко́смос — *space, cosmos*
кот — *cat (male)*
котле́та — *cutlet*
ко́фе — *coffee*
ко́шка — *cat (female)*
краси́вый — *beautiful*
кри́тик — *critic*
кста́ти — *by the way*
кто — *who*
Ку́ба — *Cuba*
куда́ — *where to*
куда́хтать — *cackle*
культу́ра — *culture*
купи́ть — *to buy*
ку́рочка — *hen (diminutive)*
курс — *course*
куса́ть — *to bite*

Л

лабора́нт — *laboratory assistant*
лаборато́рия — *laboratory*
ла́мпа — *lamp*
ле́ди — *lady*
ле́кция — *lecture*
лете́ть — *to fly*
ле́тний — *summer (adjective), summery*
ле́то — *summer*
лимо́н — *lemon*
лингви́стика — *linguistics*
лингвисти́ческий — *linguistic*
Литва́ — *Lithuania*
литерату́ра — *literature*

литерату́рный — *literature (adjective), literary*

лито́вский — *Lithuanian*

лицо́ — *face*

лоб — *forehead*

ло́жка — *spoon*

Ло́ндон — *London*

лук — *onion*

лы́жи — *skiing*

люби́мый — *favorite*

люби́ть — *to love*

любо́вь — *love*

любо́й — *any, anybody*

лю́ди — *people*

люк — *manhole*

лягу́шка — *frog*

М

магази́н — *store*

май — *May*

ма́ленький — *little, small*

ма́ма — *mom*

март — *March*

ма́сло — *butter*

мат — *swearing, filthy language*

матема́тика — *mathematics*

математи́ческий — *mathematical*

махну́ть — *to wave, flap*

маши́на — *car*

мёд — *honey*

медици́на — *medicine*

медици́нский — *medical*

ме́дленно — *slowly*

ме́дленный — *slow*

междунаро́дные отноше́ния — *international relations*

междунаро́дный — *international*

Ме́ксика — *Mexico*

мел — *chalk*

мель — *shoal*

ме́неджер — *manager*

ме́ра — *measure*

местоиме́ние — *pronoun*

ме́сяц — *month*

метро́ — *metro*

министе́рство — *ministry*

мини́стр — *minister*

мину́та — *minute*

мир — *world; peace*

мла́дший — *younger*

мно́жественное число́ — *plural number*

мо́да — *fashion*

мо́жно — *one may, one can, it's possible*

мой — *my*

мо́лодость — *youth*

молоко́ — *milk*

Москва́ — *Moscow*

муж — *husband*

музе́й — *museum*

му́зыка — *music*

музыка́льный — *music (adjective), musical*

музыка́нт — *musician*

музыкове́дение — *musicology, music history*

мы — *we*

мысль — *thought*

мыть — *to wash*

мы́шка — *little mouse*

мэр — *mayor*

мю́зикл — *musical*

мя́со — *meat*

Н

на — *on*

наве́рное — *certainly*

наза́д — *back*

называ́ть — *to call*
напи́ток — *drink*
наприме́р — *for example*
наро́дный — *folk, national*
нача́ть — *to begin*
наш — *our*
не — *not*
неда́вно — *recently, lately*
недалеко́ — *not far*
неде́ля — *week*
неме́цкий — *German*
немно́го — *a little, not many*
непло́хо — *not bad; quite well*
непра́вильно — *not right*
неро́вно — *unevenly, roughly*
нет — *no*
никогда́ — *never*
но — *but*
но́вости — *news*
но́вый — *new*
нога́ — *leg, foot*
нож — *knife*
но́мер — *number*
норма́льно — *it's all right*
ночева́ть — *to spend the night*
ночно́й — *night (adjective)*
ночь — *night*
но́чью — *at night*
ноя́брь — *November*
ну — *well (particle)*
ну́жно — *need, needed*

О

о (об) — *about*
образе́ц — *model, sample*
образова́ние — *education*
общежи́тие — *dormitory*
объе́кт — *object*
объём — *volume*
объе́хать — *go around (by vehicle)*
о́вощи — *vegetables*
овся́ная ка́ша — *oatmeal porridge*
огоро́д — *garden*
оде́жда — *clothes*
оди́н — *one*
оди́ннадцать — *eleven*
окно́ — *window*
октя́брь — *October*
он — *he*
она́ — *she*
они́ — *they*
оно́ — *it*
опа́сный — *dangerous*
о́пера — *opera*
о́пять — *again*
орёл — *eagle*
оса́ — *wasp*
осе́нний — *autumn (adjective)*
о́сень — *autumn, fall*
основно́й — *main, basic*
о́стров — *island*
отве́т — *answer*
отвеча́ть — *to answer*
отдыха́ть — *to rest, relax*
оте́ц — *father*
отку́да — *where from*
отли́чно — *excellent, perfect*
отмеча́ть — *to mark, note, celebrate*
отноше́ние — *relationship*
Отта́ва — *Ottawa*
о́фис — *office*
официа́льный — *official*
о́чень — *very*
очки́ — *glasses*
ошиба́ться — *to make mistakes*
оши́бка — *mistake*

П

паде́ж — *case (grammar term)*
пальто́ — *overcoat*
па́па — *dad*
пар — *steam*
па́спорт — *passport*
пев́ец — *singer (male)*
певи́ца — *singer (female)*
педаго́гика — *pedagogy*
педагоги́ческий — *pedagogical*
пе́рвый — *first*
перево́д — *translation*
перево́дчик — *translator*
пе́сня — *song*
петь — *to sing*
пиани́но — *piano*
пи́во — *beer*
писа́тель — *writer*
писа́тельница — *writer (female)*
писа́ть — *to write*
пистоле́т — *handgun, pistol*
письмо́ — *letter*
пить — *to drink*
пла́кать — *to cry*
план — *plan*
плати́ть — *to pay*
пла́тье — *dress*
плащ — *cloak, long raincoat*
пло́хо — *poorly, bad*
плохо́й — *bad*
пло́щадь — *square*
плыть — *to sale, swim*
пляса́ть — *to dance, hop*
по — *by*
по-америка́нски — *the American way*
по-англи́йски — *in English*
по-ара́бски — *in Arabic*
побе́да — *victory*
повторя́ть — *to repeat, review*
поговори́ть — *to talk, have a chat*
подоко́нник — *windowsill*
подраба́тывать — *to work part time*
подру́га — *friend (female), girlfriend*
по́езд — *train*
Пожа́луйста! — *1) You are welcome!; 2) please*
по́здно — *late*
познако́миться — *to meet, get acquainted with*
по-испа́нски — *in Spanish*
по-италья́нски — *in Italian*
Пока́! — *Bye!*
по-кана́дски — *the Canadian way*
по-ки́евски — *the Kiev way*
по-кита́йски — *in Chinese*
поку́пка — *purchase*
поку́почка — *purchase (diminutive)*
по́ле — *field*
поле́зный — *useful*
полёт — *flight*
поликли́ника — *policlinic*
поли́тика — *politics*
по-лито́вски — *in Lithuanian*
политологи́ческий — *Political Science (adjective)*
политоло́гия — *Political Science*
получа́ть — *to get, receive*
По́льша — *Poland*
полюби́ть — *to fall in love*
по́мнить — *to remember*
помога́ть — *to help*
по-моско́вски — *the Moscow way*
по-настоя́щему — *truly*
понеде́льник — *Monday*
по-неме́цки — *in German*
понима́ть — *to understand*

по-но́вому — *in a new way*
попуга́й — *parrot*
попуга́ть — *to frighten, startle*
популя́рный — *popular*
по-ру́сски — *in Russian*
после́дний — *last, latest*
посло́вица — *proverb*
посмотре́ть — *to look at*
посу́да — *dishes*
пото́м — *after, then*
потому́ что — *because*
по-украи́нски — *in Ukrainian*
по-францу́зски — *in French*
похо́ж — *look like, resemble*
почему́ — *why*
поэ́т — *poet*
по-япо́нски — *in Japan*
пра́вда — *truth*
пра́вило — *rule*
пра́вильно — *correct, right*
пра́во — *right*
правосла́вный — *orthodox*
пра́здник — *holiday, celebration*
пра́здновать — *to celebrate*
предло́г — *preposition*
предложе́ние — *sentence*
предло́жный — *prepositional*
предме́т — *1) object; 2) school subject*
президе́нт — *president*
преподава́тель — *instructor, professor*
преподава́тельница — *instructor, professor (female)*
Приве́т! — *Hi!*
прилага́тельное — *adjective*
приходи́ть — *to come over*
прия́тно — *it's a pleasure*
прия́тный — *pleasant, enjoyable*
про — *about (+Acc. case)*
пробле́ма — *problem*
продаве́ц — *shop assistant*
продавщи́ца — *shop assistant (female)*
проза́ик — *prose writer, novelist*
проси́ть — *to ask for a favor*
проспе́кт — *avenue*
про́сто — *simply*
просто́й — *simple*
профе́ссия — *profession*
профе́ссор — *professor*
пря́мо — *straight*
психологи́ческий — *psychological*
психоло́гия — *psychology*
пти́ца — *bird*
пульс — *pulse*
пчела́ — *bee*
пчёлка — *bee (diminutive)*
пятна́дцать — *fifteen*
пя́тница — *Friday*
пя́тый — *fifth*
пять — *five*
пятьдеся́т — *fifty*

Р

рабо́та — *work*
рабо́тать — *to work*
рабо́чий — *1) worker; 2) working*
рад — *glad*
ра́дио — *radio*
разби́ть — *break, crack*
разби́ться — *to get broken, cracked*
ра́зный — *different*
ра́ньше — *before, earlier*
расска́з — *story*
расска́зывать — *to tell a story*
ребёнок — *child*
ребя́та — *kids, guys*
ре́дко — *rarely*

религио́зный — *religious*
рестора́н — *restaurant*
рис — *rice*
род — *gender, kinship*
родно́й — *native*
Рождество́ — *Christmas*
рок — *rock*
рома́н — *novel*
Росси́йская Импе́рия — *Russian Empire*
Росси́йская Федера́ция — *The Russian Federation*
росси́йский — *Russian*
Росси́я — *Russia*
россия́нин — *Russian citizen (male)*
россия́нка — *Russian citizen (female)*
рот — *mouth*
РСФСР (Росси́йская Сове́тская Федерати́вная Социалисти́ческая Респу́блика) — *The Russian Soviet Federative Socialist Republic*
руга́ться — *swear, curse*
рука́ — *hand*
ру́сский — *Russian*
Русь — *Rus"*
ру́чка — *pen*
ры́ба — *fish*
рюкза́к — *backpack*

С

с — *with*
саксофо́н — *saxophone*
са́мый — *the most*
са́хар — *sugar*
свобо́дно — *freely, fluently*
свой — *one's own*
сда́ча — *change*
себя́ — *yourself*
се́вер — *north*
сего́дня — *today*
сейча́с — *now*
секрета́рь — *secretary*
семе́йный — *family (adjective)*
семе́стр — *semester, term*
семна́дцать — *seventeen*
семь — *seven*
се́мьдесят — *seventy*
семья́ — *family*
сентя́брь — *September*
серьёзный — *serious*
сестра́ — *sister*
сесть — *to sit*
си́ла — *strength, power*
сказа́ть — *to say*
ска́зка — *fairy tale*
ско́лько — *how many, how much*
ску́чно — *it's boring*
ску́чный — *boring*
слави́стика — *Slavic Studies*
сла́дости — *sweets*
сли́вки — *cream*
слова́рь — *dictionary*
сло́во — *word*
слу́шать — *to listen*
смешно́й — *funny*
смотре́ть — *to watch, look at*
снег — *snow*
снести́ — *to lay (an egg)*
соба́ка — *dog*
сова́ — *owl*
сове́тский — *Soviet*
совреме́нный — *contemporary, modern*
сок — *juice*
сон — *dream*
со́рок — *forty*
социологи́ческий — *sociological*
социоло́гия — *Social Science, sociology*

Спаси́бо! — *Thank you!*
спать — *to sleep*
Споко́йной но́чи! — *Good night!*
спо́рить — *to argue*
спортза́л — *gym*
спортсме́н — *athlete*
спортсме́нка — *athlete (female)*
среда́ — *Wednesday*
сре́дний — *middle*
СССР (Сою́з Советских Социалисти́ческих Респу́блик) — *USSR (Union of Soviet Socialist Republics)*
стака́н — *glass*
ста́рший — *older*
ста́рый — *old*
стати́стика — *statistics*
статья́ — *article*
сто — *one hundred*
столи́ца — *capital*
стоя́ть — *to stand*
страна́ — *country*
страни́ца — *page*
стро́чка — *line*
студе́нт — *student (male)*
студе́нтка — *student (female)*
сты́дно — *shame*
суббо́та — *Saturday*
субти́тры — *subtitles*
Су́здаль — *Suzdal*
суп — *soup*
су́ши — *sushi*
США (Соединённые Шта́ты Аме́рики) — *USA (United States of America)*
съесть — *to have eaten up*
сын — *son*
сыр — *cheese*
сюрпри́з — *surprise*

Т

та́кже — *also*
тако́й — *such*
такси́ — *taxi*
тала́нтливо — *skillfully, with talent*
тала́нтливый — *talented*
там — *there*
танцо́р — *dancer*
таре́лка — *plate*
твой — *your, yours*
теа́тр — *theatre*
текст — *text*
телеви́дение — *TV broadcast, television*
телеви́зор — *TV, television set*
телефо́н — *telephone*
те́ло — *body*
те́ма — *theme, topic*
теннеси́ст — *tennis player (male)*
теннеси́стка — *tennis player (female)*
тепе́рь — *now*
терапе́вт — *physician*
тест — *test*
тетра́дь — *notebook*
тётя — *aunt*
те́хника — *technology*
тип — *type*
тихи́й — *quiet*
това́рищ — *comrade, a friend*
тогда́ — *then*
то́же — *also*
то́лько — *only*
том — *volume, part*
тот — *that*
то́чка — *dot, point*
тре́тий — *third*
три — *three*
три́дцать — *thirty*
трина́дцать — *thirteen*

тромбо́н — *trombone*
труд — *work, labor*
тру́дно — *it's difficult, hard*
тру́дный — *difficult, hard*
туристи́ческая фи́рма — *travel agency*
туристи́ческий — *tourist (adjective)*
турфи́рма — *travel agency*
Ту́рция — *Turkey*
тут — *here*
ту́фли — *shoes*
ты — *you (singular, informal)*

У

у — *at*
у́гол — *corner*
у́голь — *coal*
удиви́тельно — *amazingly, surprisingly*
уже́ — *already*
у́жин — *dinner, supper*
узна́ть — *to find out, learn*
украи́нский — *Ukrainian*
у́лица — *street*
ум — *mind, intellect*
у́мный — *smart*
университе́т — *university*
упа́сть — *to fall down*
упражне́ние — *exercise*
уро́к — *lesson*
уста́вший (уста́ть) — *tired*
у́тром — *in the morning*
уха́ — *fresh fish soup*
у́хо (pl.: у́ши) — *ear*
учёба — *studies*
уче́бник — *textbook*
учени́к — *pupil*
учёный — *scientist*
учи́тель — *teacher*
учи́тельница — *teacher (female)*
учи́ть — *1) to learn, memorize; 2) to teach*
учи́ться — *to study, be a student*

Ф

фа́за — *phase*
факульте́т — *faculty*
февра́ль — *February*
фе́рма — *farm*
фе́рмер — *farmer*
фигури́ст — *figure skater (male)*
фигури́стка — *figure skater (female)*
фи́зика — *physics*
физи́ческий — *physical, physics (adjective)*
филологи́ческий — *philological*
филоло́гия — *philology*
фило́соф — *philosopher*
филосо́фия — *philosophy*
филосо́фский — *philosophical*
фина́нсы — *finance*
фи́рма — *firm*
фи́тнес — *fitness, fitness centre*
фле́йта — *flute*
фонта́н — *fountain*
фо́то — *photo*
фотоаппара́т — *photo camera*
Фра́нция — *France*
францу́зский — *French*
фру́кты — *fruit*
футбо́л — *soccer*

Х

хво́стик — *tail*
хи́мия — *chemistry*
хлеб — *bread*
хоро́ший — *good*
хорошо́ — *well*
хоте́ть — *to want*
христиа́не — *Christians*

Ц

це́литься — *to aim*

це́рковь — *church*

цирк — *circus*

ци́фра — *figure, digit*

Ч

чай — *tea*

ча́йник — *teapot*

час — *hour*

ча́сто — *often*

часть — *part*

часы́ — *watch*

ча́шка — *cup*

чей (чья, чьё, чьи) — *whose*

челове́к — *person*

четве́рг — *Thursday*

четвёртый — *fourth*

четы́ре — *four*

четы́рнадцать — *fourteen*

Че́хия — *Czech Republic*

числи́тельное — *numeral*

число́ — *number*

чита́ть — *to read*

что — *what*

Ш

ша́пка — *hat*

шар — *sphere, globe*

шарф — *scarf*

шестна́дцать — *sixteen*

шесто́й — *sixth*

шесть — *six*

шестьдеся́т — *sixty*

шко́ла — *school*

шко́льник — *schoolboy*

шко́льница — *schoolgirl*

шокола́д — *chocolate*

шо́рты — *shorts*

шу́тка — *joke*

Щ

щи — *cabbage soup*

Э

экза́мен — *exam*

эконо́мика — *economy*

экономи́ческий — *economic*

экску́рсия — *excursion*

электри́чка — *suburban electric train*

э́то — *this is*

э́хо — *echo*

Ю

юг — *south*

юриди́ческая фи́рма — *law firm*

юриди́ческий — *law (adjective), legal*

юриспруде́нция (правове́дение) — *jurisprudence, law*

юри́ст — *lawyer*

Я

я — *I*

я́блоко — *apple*

язы́к — *language, tongue*

яи́чко — *egg (diminutive)*

янва́рь — *January*

Япо́ния — *Japan*

япо́нский — *Japanese*

Англо-русский словарь

A

actress — *актри́са*
adjective — *прилага́тельное*
adult — *взро́слый*
after, then — *пото́м*
again — *о́пять*
aim — *це́литься*
Alaska — *Аля́ска*
all — *все*
all, entire — *весь*
already — *уже́*
also — *та́кже*
also — *то́же*
amazingly — *удиви́тельно*
America — *Аме́рика*
American — *америка́нский*
American way — *по-америка́нски*
and — *да (и)*
and — *и*
animal — *живо́тное*
another — *друго́й*
answer — *отве́т*
answer — *отвеча́ть*
anthropology — *антрополо́гия*
any, anybody — *любо́й*
apartment — *кварти́ра*
apple — *я́блоко*
April — *апре́ль*
Arabic — *ара́бский*
archeology — *археоло́гия*
architecture — *архитекту́ра*
Argentina — *Аргенти́на*
argue — *спо́рить*
art studies — *искусствове́дение*
article — *статья́*
ask for a favor — *проси́ть*
astronaut, cosmonaut — *космона́вт*
at — *у*
at home — *до́ма*
at night — *но́чью*
At what time? — *Во ско́лько?*
athlete — *спортсме́н, спортсме́нка (female)*
atom — *а́том*
August — *а́вгуст*
aunt — *тётя*
Australia — *Австра́лия*
autumn (adjective) — *осе́нний*
autumn, fall — *о́сень*
avenue — *проспе́кт*
awesome, cool — *здо́рово*

B

back — *наза́д*
backpack — *рюкза́к*
bad — *плохо́й*
ballerina — *балери́на*
ballet — *бале́т*
banana — *бана́н*
bank — *банк*
bar — *бар*
bathtub — *ва́нна*
be — *быть*
beat — *би́ться*
beat — *бить*
beautiful — *краси́вый*
because — *потому́ что*
bee — *пчела́, пчёлка (diminutive)*
beer — *пи́во*
before — *ра́ньше*

begin — *начáть*
bicycle — *велосипéд*
big — *большóй*
biology — *биолóгия*
bird — *птúца*
Birthday — *День рождéния*
bite — *кусáть*
blues — *блюз*
body — *тéло*
book — *кнúга*
boring — *скýчный*
borsch — *борщ*
bread — *хлеб*
break, crack — *разбúть*
brother — *брат*
buffet (cafeteria) — *буфéт*
building — *здáние*
Bulgaria — *Болгáрия*
bus — *автóбус*
businessman — *бизнесмéн*
but — *но, а*
butter — *мáсло*
buy — *купúть*
by — *по*
by way — *кстáти*
Bye! — *Покá!*

C

cabbage soup — *щи*
cackle — *кудáхтать*
cafe — *кафé*
calendar — *календáрь*
call — *звать*
call — *называ́ть*
Canada — *Канáда*
Canadian — *канáдский*
Canadian way — *по-канáдски*
capital — *столúца*
car — *машúна*
case — *падéж (grammar term)*
cat — *кóшка (female); кот (male)*
celebrate — *прáздновать, отмечáть*
century — *век*
certainly — *навéрное*
chalk — *мел*
change — *сдáча*
cheap — *дешёвый*
cheerful — *весёлый*
cheerfully — *вéсело*
cheese — *сыр*
chemistry — *хúмия*
child — *ребёнок*
children — *дéти*
children's — *дéтский*
China — *Китáй*
Chinese — *китáйский*
chocolate — *шоколáд*
choose — *выбирáть*
Christians — *христиáне*
Christmas — *Рождествó*
church — *цéрковь*
circus — *цирк*
citizen — *граждани́н*
city — *гóрод*
clarinet — *кларнéт*
class — *занятие*
class — *класс*
classical — *классúческий*
cloak — *плащ*
close — *блúзко*
clothes — *одéжда*
club — *клуб*
coal — *ýголь*
coffee — *кóфе*
college — *кóлледж*
come over — *приходúть*

command — *кома́нда*
comment — *коммента́рий*
commercial firm — *комме́рческая фи́рма*
company — *компа́ния*
composer — *компози́тор*
computer — *компьютер, компью́терный (adjective)*
computer equipment — *компью́терная те́хника*
computer science — *информа́тика*
comrade, a friend — *това́рищ*
concert — *конце́рт*
conservatory — *консервато́рия*
contemporary, modern — *совреме́нный*
cool, awesome — *кла́ссно*
corner — *у́гол*
correct, right — *пра́вильно*
country — *страна́*
course — *курс*
cream — *сли́вки*
critic — *кри́тик*
cry — *пла́кать*
Cuba — *Ку́ба*
culture — *культу́ра*
cup — *ча́шка*
cutlet — *котле́та*
Czech Republic — *Че́хия*

D

dad — *па́па*
dance (hop) — *пляса́ть*
dancer — *танцо́р*
dangerous — *опа́сный*
daughter — *дочь, до́чка (diminutive)*
day off — *выходно́й*
dear — *дорого́й*
December — *дека́брь*
defense — *защи́та*
Denmark — *Да́ния*
department — *ка́федра*
dialogue — *диало́г*
dictionary — *слова́рь*
different — *ра́зный*
difficult — *тру́дный*
dinner (supper) — *у́жин*
dishes — *посу́да*
do, make — *де́лать*
doctor — *врач*
dog — *соба́ка*
dormitory — *общежи́тие*
dot, point — *то́чка*
down — *вниз*
dream — *сон*
dress — *пла́тье*
drink — *напи́ток, to drink — пить*
drive — *е́хать*

E

eagle — *орёл*
ear — *у́хо (pl.: у́ши)*
east — *восто́к*
eat — *есть*
echo — *э́хо*
economic — *экономи́ческий*
economy — *эконо́мика*
education — *образова́ние*
egg — *яйцо, яи́чко (diminutive)*
eight — *во́семь*
eighteen — *восемна́дцать*
eighty — *во́семьдесят*
eleven — *оди́ннадцать*
else — *ещё*
engineer — *инжене́р, инжене́рный (adjective)*
England — *Англия*
English — *англи́йский*

entrance — *вход*
Europe — *Европа*
even — *даже*
evening — *вечер*
Everything is all right! — *Всё в порядке!*
everything — *всё*
exam — *экзамен*
excellent — *отлично*
excursion — *экскурсия*
Excuse me — *Извините*
exercise — *упражнение*
expensive — *дорогой*
eye — *глаз (pl. глаза)*

F

face — *лицо*
faculty — *факультет*
fairy tale — *сказка*
fall down — *упасть*
fall in love — *полюбить*
family — *семья, семейный (adjective)*
far — *далеко*
farm — *ферма*
farmer — *фермер*
fashion — *мода*
fast, quick — *быстрый*
fast, quickly — *быстро*
father — *отец*
favorite — *любимый*
February — *февраль*
feminine — *женский*
field — *поле*
fifteen — *пятнадцать*
fifth — *пятый*
fifty — *пятьдесят*
figure skater — *фигурист (male), фигуристка (female)*
figure (digit) — *цифра*
finance — *финансы*
find out — *узнать*
firm — *фирма*
first — *первый*
fir-tree — *ёлка*
fish — *рыба*
fitness — *фитнес*
five — *пять*
flight — *полёт*
fluently — *свободно*
flute — *флейта*
fly — *лететь*
folk (national) — *народный*
food — *еда*
foot — *нога*
for — *за*
for example — *например*
forehead — *лоб*
foreign — *иностранный*
fork — *вилка*
forty — *сорок*
fountain — *фонтан*
four — *четыре*
fourteen — *четырнадцать*
fourth — *четвёртый*
France — *Франция*
free of charge — *бесплатно*
freely — *свободно*
French — *французский*
fresh fish soup — *уха*
Friday — *пятница*
friend — *друг (male), подруга (female) (pl.: друзья)*
friendship — *дружба*
frighten — *попугать*
frog — *лягушка*
from — *из*
fruit — *фрукты*

funny — *смешно́й*
future — *бу́дущий*

G

garden — *огоро́д*
gender studies — *ге́ндерные иссле́дования*
gender — *род*
geography — *геогра́фия*
geology — *геоло́гия*
German — *неме́цкий*
Germany — *Герма́ния*
get — *получа́ть*
get acquainted with — *познако́миться*
get broken (cracked) — *разби́ться*
get-together party — *вечери́нка*
girlfriend — *подру́га*
give — *дать*
glad — *рад*
glass — *стака́н*
glasses — *очки́*
go around (by vehicle) — *объе́хать*
go by a vehicle — *е́хать*
go (by foot) — *идти́*
golden — *золото́й*
good — *хоро́ший*
Good afternoon! — *До́брый день!*
Good morning! — *До́брое у́тро!*
Good morning! — *До́брый ве́чер!*
Good night! — *Споко́йной но́чи!*
Goodbye! — *До свида́ния!*
graduate school — *аспиранту́ра*
graduate student — *аспира́нт (male), аспира́нтка (female)*
grammar — *грамма́тика*
grandfather — *дед*
grandpa — *де́душка*
grandmother (grandma, granny) — *ба́бушка*
Greece — *Гре́ция*
group — *гру́ппа*
guest — *гость*
guitar — *гита́ра*
guitar player — *гитари́ст*
gym — *спортза́л*
gymnast — *гимна́ст (male), гимна́стка (female)*

H

hand — *рука́*
handgun (pistol) — *пистоле́т*
hat — *ша́пка*
have completed learning — *вы́учиться*
have eaten up — *съесть*
he — *он*
head — *голова́*
heat — *жар*
Hello! — *Здра́вствуйте!*
help — *помога́ть*
hen — *ку́рочка (diminutive)*
her — *её*
here — *здесь, тут*
here it is — *вот*
Hi! — *Приве́т!*
his — *его́*
history — *исто́рия*
historical — *истори́ческий*
holiday — *пра́здник*
home — *дом, дома́шний (adjective); домо́й (answers куда́? — where to?)*
honey — *мёд*
hospital — *больни́ца*
hour — *час*
house — *дом*

how — *как*
How are you? — *Как дела́?*
How is life? — *Как жизнь?*
how many — *ско́лько*
how much — *ско́лько*
Humanities, humanitarian — *гуманита́рный*
husband — *муж*

I

I — *я*
idea — *иде́я*
if — *е́сли*
important — *ва́жный*
in a new way — *по-но́вому*
in afternoon — *днём*
in Arabic — *по-ара́бски*
in Chinese — *по-кита́йски*
in English — *по-англи́йски*
in evening — *ве́чером*
in French — *по-францу́зски*
in German — *по-неме́цки*
in Italian — *по-италья́нски*
in Japan — *по-япо́нски*
in Lithuanian — *по-лито́вски*
in morning — *у́тром*
in Russian — *по-ру́сски*
in Spanish — *по-испа́нски*
in Ukrainian — *по-украи́нски*
in (at) — *в*
institute — *институ́т*
instructor — *преподава́тель (male), преподава́тельница (female)*
intellect — *ум*
interesting — *интере́сный*
international — *междунаро́дный*
international relations — *междунаро́дные отноше́ния*
internet — *Интерне́т*
island — *о́стров*
it — *оно́ (also: он, она for objects)*
it is interesting — *интере́сно*
Italian — *италья́нский*
Italy — *Ита́лия*
it's a pleasure — *прия́тно*
it's all right — *норма́льно*
it's boring — *ску́чно*
it's difficult — *тру́дно*
it's important — *ва́жно*

J

January — *янва́рь*
Japan — *Япо́ния*
Japanese — *япо́нский*
jazz — *джаз*
joke — *шу́тка*
journal (magazine) — *журна́л*
journalism — *журнали́стика*
journalist — *журнали́ст, журнали́стка (female)*
juice — *сок*
July — *ию́ль*
June — *ию́нь*
jurisprudence — *юриспруде́нция, правове́дение*

K

kangaroo — *кенгуру́*
kids, guys — *ребя́та*
Kiev way — *по-ки́евски*
kind — *до́брый*
king — *коро́ль*
knife — *нож*
know — *знать*

L

laboratory — *лаборатóрия*
laboratory assistant — *лаборáнт, лаборáнтка (female)*
lady — *лéди*
lamp — *лáмпа*
language — *язы́к*
last (latest) — *послéдний*
late — *пóздно*
legal — *юриди́ческий*
law firm — *юриди́ческая фи́рма*
lawyer — *юри́ст*
lay (an egg) — *снести́*
learn — *учи́ть*
learn (have learned) — *вы́учить*
lecture — *лéкция*
lecture (class) room– аудитóрия
leg — *ногá*
lemon — *лимóн*
lesson — *урóк*
letter — *письмó*
letter (character) — *бýква*
librarian — *библиотéкарь*
library — *библиотéка, библиотéчный (adjective)*
life — *жизнь*
line — *стрóчка*
linguistic — *лингвисти́ческий*
linguistics — *лингви́стика*
listen — *слýшать*
literature — *литератýра*
literary — *литератýрный*
Lithuania — *Литвá*
Lithuanian — *литóвский*
little small — *мáленький*
live — *жить*
live through winter — *зимовáть*
London — *Лóндон*
long — *дли́нный*
long ago — *давнó*
look at — *посмотрéть*
look like — *похóж*
loudly — *грóмко*
love — *любóвь, to love — люби́ть*

M

main — *основнóй*
make mistakes — *ошибáться*
manager — *мéнеджер*
manhole — *люк*
March — *март*
mark (celebrate) — *отмечáть*
mathematical — *математи́ческий*
mathematics — *матемáтика*
May — *май*
may (can) — *мóжно*
mayor — *мэр*
mean — *знáчить*
measure — *мéра*
meat — *мя́со*
medical — *меди́цинский*
medicine — *медици́на*
meet — *встрéтиться*
meet (get acquainted with) — *познакóмиться*
metro — *метрó*
Mexico — *Мéксика*
middle — *срéдний*
milk — *молокó*
mind — *ум*
minister — *мини́стр*
ministry — *министéрство*
minute — *минýта*
mistake — *оши́бка*
model (sample) — *образéц*
mom — *мáма*

Monday — *понеде́льник*
month — *ме́сяц*
more (else) — *ещё*
Moscow — *Москва́*
Moscow way — *по-моско́вски*
mosquito — *кома́р*
most — *са́мый*
mouse — *мышь, мы́шка (diminutive)*
mouth — *рот*
movie, movies — *кино́*
museum — *музе́й*
music — *му́зыка*
musical — *мю́зикл, музыка́льный (adjective)*
musician — *музыка́нт*
musicology — *музыкове́дение*
my — *мой (моя, моё, мои)*

N

nail — *гвоздь*
naked — *го́лый*
native — *родно́й*
need, needed — *ну́жно*
never — *никогда́*
new — *но́вый*
news — *но́вости*
newspaper — *газе́та*
night — *ночь, ночно́й (adjective)*
nine — *де́вять*
nineteen — *девятна́дцать*
ninety — *девяно́сто*
no — *нет*
north — *се́вер*
not — *не*
not bad (quite well) — *непло́хо*
not far — *недалеко́*
not right — *непра́вильно*
notebook — *тетра́дь*
novel — *рома́н*
November — *ноя́брь*
now — *сейча́с, тепе́рь*
number — *но́мер, число́*
numeral — *числи́тельное*

O

oatmeal porridge — *овся́ная ка́ша*
object — *предме́т, объе́кт*
occupation — *заня́тие*
October — *октя́брь*
of course — *коне́чно*
office — *о́фис*
official — *официа́льный*
often — *ча́сто*
old — *ста́рый*
older — *ста́рший*
on — *на*
once upon a time (lived and were) — *жи́ли-бы́ли*
one — *оди́н*
one hundred — *сто*
one may (one can, it's possible) — *мо́жно*
one's own — *свой*
onion — *лук*
only — *то́лько*
opera — *о́пера*
or — *и́ли*
orange — *апельси́н*
orthodox — *правосла́вный*
Ottawa — *Отта́ва*
our — *наш*
overcoat — *пальто́*
owl — *сова́*

P

page — *страни́ца*
paper — *бума́га*

parrot — *попуга́й*
part — *часть*
passport — *па́спорт*
pay — *плати́ть*
peace — *мир*
peasant woman (granny) — *ба́ба*
pedagogical — *педагоги́ческий*
pedagogy — *педаго́гика*
pen — *ру́чка*
pencil — *каранда́ш*
people — *лю́ди*
person — *челове́к*
phase — *фа́за*
philological — *филологи́ческий*
philology — *филоло́гия*
philosopher — *фило́соф*
philosophical — *философ́ский*
philosophy — *филосо́фия*
photo camera — *фотоаппара́т*
photo — *фо́то*
physical — *физи́ческий*
physics — *фи́зика, физи́ческий (adjective)*
physician — *терапе́вт*
physics — *фи́зика*
piano — *пиани́но*
plan — *план*
plant (factory) — *заво́д*
plate — *таре́лка*
play — *игра́ть*
play an instrument — *игра́ть на*
playwright — *драмату́рг*
pleasant — *прия́тный*
please — *пожа́луйста*
plural number — *мно́жественное число́*
poet — *поэ́т*
Poland — *По́льша*
policlinic — *поликли́ника*
Political Science — *политоло́гия,* политологи́ческий (adjective)
politics — *поли́тика*
poorly — *пло́хо*
popular — *популя́рный*
potatoes — *карто́фель*
preposition — *предло́г*
prepositional — *предло́жный*
president — *президе́нт*
problem — *пробле́ма*
profession — *профе́ссия*
professor — *профе́ссор*
pronoun — *местоиме́ние*
prose writer — *проза́ик*
proverb — *посло́вица*
psychological — *психологи́ческий*
psychology — *психоло́гия*
pulse — *пульс*
pupil — *учени́к*
purchase — *поку́пка, поку́почка (diminutive)*

Q

question — *вопро́с*
quiet — *тихи́й*

R

radio — *ра́дио*
railway station — *вокза́л*
rain — *дождь*
rarely — *ре́дко*
read — *чита́ть*
recall (recollect, remember) — *вспо́мнить*
recently — *неда́вно*
relationship — *отноше́ние*
religious — *религио́зный*
remember — *по́мнить*
remember (keep in mind) — *запо́мнить*
repeat — *повторя́ть*

research — *исслéдование*
resemble — *похóж*
rest — *отдыхáть*
restaurant — *ресторáн*
resurrect — *воскреси́ть*
review — *повторя́ть*
rice — *рис*
right — *прáво*
road — *дорóга*
rock — *рок*
room — *кóмната*
rule — *прáвило*
run — *бежáть*
Rus' — *Русь*
Russia — *Росси́я*
Russian — *росси́йский, рýсский*
Russian citizen — *россия́нин (male), россия́нка*
Russian Empire — *Росси́йская Импéрия*
Russian Federation — *Росси́йская Федерáция*
Russian Soviet Federative Socialist Republic — *РСФСР (Росси́йская Совéтская Федерати́вная Социалисти́ческая Респýблика)*

S

sale — *плыть*
Saturday — *суббóта*
sausage — *колбасá*
saxophone — *саксофóн*
say — *сказáть*
scarf — *шарф*
school — *шкóла*
school subject — *предмéт*
schoolboy — *шкóльник*
schoolgirl — *шкóльница*
scientist — *учёный*
season — *врéмя гóда*
second — *вторóй*
secretary — *секретáрь*
See you tomorrow! — *До зáвтра!*
See you! (Until we meet!) — *До встрéчи!*
seem — *казáться*
semester — *семéстр*
sentence — *предложéние*
September — *сентя́брь*
serious — *серьёзный*
seven — *семь*
seventeen — *семнáдцать*
seventy — *сéмьдесят*
shame — *сты́дно*
she — *онá*
shoal — *мель*
shoes — *тýфли*
shop assistant — *продавéц, продавщи́ца (female)*
shorts — *шóрты*
simple — *простóй*
simply — *прóсто*
sing — *петь*
singer — *певéц (male), певи́ца (female)*
sister — *сестрá*
sit — *сесть*
six — *шесть*
sixteen — *шестнáдцать*
sixth — *шестóй*
sixty — *шестьдеся́т*
skiing — *лы́жи*
skillfully (with talent) — *талáнтливо*
Slavic Studies — *слави́стика*
sleep — *спать*
slow — *мéдленный*
slowly — *мéдленно*
small — *мáленький*
smart — *ýмный*

snow — *снег*
soccer — *футбо́л*
Social Science (sociology) — *социоло́гия*
sociological — *социологи́ческий*
sometimes — *иногда́*
son — *сын*
song — *пе́сня*
sorrow — *грусть*
sound — *звук*
soup — *суп*
south — *юг*
Soviet — *сове́тский*
space station — *косми́ческая ста́нция*
space (cosmos) — *ко́смос*
Spain — *Испа́ния*
Spanish — *испа́нский*
speak — *говори́ть*
spend night — *ночева́ть*
sphere (globe) — *шар*
spoon — *ло́жка*
spring — *весна́, весе́нний (adjective)*
square — *пло́щадь*
stand — *стоя́ть*
statistics — *стати́стика*
steam — *пар*
stomach — *живо́т*
store — *магази́н*
story — *расска́з*
straight — *пря́мо*
street — *у́лица*
strength — *си́ла*
student — *студе́нт (male), студе́нтка (female)*
studies — *учёба*
study a subject — *изуча́ть*
study (be a student) — *учи́ться*
study (do homework) — *занима́ться*
subtitles — *субти́тры*
suburban electric train — *электри́чка*
such — *тако́й*
sugar — *са́хар*
summer — *ле́то*
summery — *ле́тний*
summer cottage — *да́ча*
Sunday — *воскресе́нье, воскре́сный (adjective)*
surely — *ве́рно*
surprise — *сюрпри́з*
sushi — *су́ши*
Suzdal — *Су́здаль*
swear — *руга́ться*
swearing — *мат*
sweets — *сла́дости*
swim — *плыть*

T

tail — *хвост, хво́стик (diminutive)*
take — *брать*
talented — *тала́нтливый*
talk (have a chat) — *поговори́ть*
taxi — *такси́*
tea — *чай*
teach — *учи́ть*
teacher — *учи́тель, учи́тельница (female)*
team — *кома́нда*
teapot — *ча́йник*
technology — *те́хника*
telephone — *телефо́н*
tell a story — *расска́зывать*
ten — *де́сять*
tennis player — *теннис́ист (male)* теннис́истка (female)
test — *тест*
text — *текст*
textbook — *уче́бник*
Thank you! — *Спаси́бо!*

that — *тот*
theatre — *теа́тр*
their — *их*
theme (topic) — *те́ма*
then — *тогда́*
there — *там*
there is — *есть*
they — *они́*
thing — *вещь*
think — *ду́мать*
third — *тре́тий*
thirteen — *трина́дцать*
thirty — *три́дцать*
this is — *э́то*
thought — *ду́ма*
thought — *мысль*
three — *три*
Thursday — *четве́рг*
time — *вре́мя*
tired — *уста́вший (from: уста́ть)*
today — *сего́дня*
tomorrow — *за́втра*
tongue — *язы́к*
tooth — *зуб*
touch — *задева́ть*
tourist — *турист, туристи́ческий (adjective)*
tourist guide — *гид-экскурсово́д*
train — *по́езд*
translation — *перево́д*
translator — *перево́дчик*
travel agency — *туристи́ческая фи́рма*
travel agency — *турфи́рма*
trombone — *тромбо́н*
truly — *по-настоя́щему*
truth — *пра́вда*
Tuesday — *вто́рник*
Turkey — *Ту́рция*
TV broadcast (television) — *телеви́дение*
TV, television set — *телеви́зор*
twelve — *двена́дцать*
twenty — *два́дцать*
two — *два*
type — *тип*

U

Ukrainian — *украи́нский*
uncle — *дя́дя*
understand — *понима́ть*
unevenly — *неро́вно*
university — *университе́т*
unlikely — *вряд ли*
until — *до*
USA — *США (Соединённые Шта́ты Аме́рики)*
useful — *поле́зный*
USSR (Union of Soviet Socialist Republics) — *СССР (Сою́з Советских Социалисти́ческих Респу́блик)*

V

vase — *ва́за*
vegetables — *о́вощи*
verb — *глаго́л*
verb of motion — *глаго́л движе́ния*
very — *о́чень*
victory — *побе́да*
vodka — *во́дка*
volume — *объём*
volume — *том*

W

want — *хоте́ть*
wash — *мыть*
washed — *вы́мыт*
Washington — *Вашингто́н*

wasp — *осá*
watch — *часы́*
watch (look at) — *смотре́ть*
water — *водá*
wave — *махну́ть*
we — *мы*
Wednesday — *средá*
week — *неде́ля*
well — *хорошó; ну (particle)*
west — *зáпад*
what — *что*
what kind — *какóй*
whatever — *всё равнó*
when — *когдá*
where — *где*
where from — *откýда*
where to — *кудá*
who — *кто*
whose — *чей (чья, чьё, чьи)*
why — *почемý*
wife — *женá*
window — *окнó*
windowsill — *подокóнник*
winter — *зимá, зи́мний (adjective)*
with — *с*
without — *без*
word — *слóво*
work — *рабóта*
work — *рабóтать*
work part time — *подрабáтывать*
work (labor) — *труд*
worker — *рабóчий*
working — *рабóчий*
world — *мир*
write — *писáть*
writer — *писáтель, писáтельница (female)*

Y

yardman — *двóрник*
year — *год*
yes — *да*
yesterday — *вчерá*
yogurt — *йóгурт*
you — *вы (plural, formal), ты (singular, informal)*
You are welcome! — *Пожáлуйста!*
younger — *млáдший*
your, yours (plural) — *ваш (вáша, вáше, вáши)*
your, yours (singular) — *твой (твоя́, твоё, твои́)*
yourself — *себя́*
youth — *мóлодость*

Photo Credits: The following photographs are taken from the Wikimedia Commons (http://commons.wikimedia.org) and released into the public domain:

page 15: the Glagolitic alphabet;

page 16: the Cyrillic alphabet;

page 16: chart with letters crossed out by Peter I;

page 45: portrait of Alexander Pushkin by Orest Kiprensky; photo of Leo Tolstoy by Sergei Prokudin-Gorsky; portrait of Fyodor Dostoyevsky by Vasily Perov; painting of Anna Akhmatova by Nathan Altman; photo of Marina Tsvetaeva; portrait of Anton Chekhov by Osip Braz; photo of Yuri Gagarin (original source: www.sydsvenskan.se);

page 108: Zemfira by Marina Zakharova; Jimmy Page (original source: www.musicroom.com).

The following images are credited to RIA Novosti archive:

page 45: M. S. Gorbachev by Vladimir Vyatkin; R. M. Gorbacheva by Boris Babanov.